AT THE DOOR

AT THE DOOR
Selected Literature for ESL Students

Sandra McKay

Dorothy Petitt

San Francisco State University

PRENTICE HALL REGENTS
Englewood Cliffs, New Jersey 07632

Library of Congress Cataloging in Publication Data

Main entry under title:
At the door.

1. English language—Text-books for foreign speakers.
2. English language—Readers—1950- . I. McKay, Sandra. II. Petitt, Dorothy.
PE1128.A69 1984 428.6'4 83-3345
ISBN 0-13-049676-6

Editorial/production supervision and
interior design: F. Hubert
Cover design: Wanda Lubelska
Manufacturing buyer: Harry P. Baisley

Prentice-Hall, Inc.
A Paramount Communications Company
Englewood Cliffs, New Jersey 07632

Printed in the United States of America

20 19 18 17 16 15 14 13 12 11

ISBN 0-13-049676-6

PRENTICE-HALL INTERNATIONAL, INC., *London*
PRENTICE-HALL OF AUSTRALIA PTY. LIMITED, *Sydney*
EDITORA PRENTICE-HALL DO BRASIL, LTDA., *Rio de Janeiro*
PRENTICE-HALL CANADA INC., *Toronto*
PRENTICE-HALL OF INDIA PRIVATE LIMITED, *New Delhi*
PRENTICE-HALL OF JAPAN, INC., *Tokyo*
PRENTICE-HALL OF SOUTHEAST ASIA PTE. LTD., *Singapore*
WHITEHALL BOOKS LIMITED, *Wellington, New Zealand*

CONTENTS

PREFACE

Why Literature?

We believe that literature offers several benefits to ESL students. First, literature offers pleasure. Because many students enjoy reading literature, they are motivated to read it, ultimately developing their reading proficiency. Second, literature offers insight into human experience; in this book, people of diverse cultural backgrounds respond to new experiences. Third, literature offers uses of language that students can learn to appreciate and use in their own writing. Finally, literature offers encouragement to ESL students to compose a record of their own experience.

Selection and Arrangement

Two criteria governed the selection of the literature included in this text. First, the literature was to be about experiences students could relate to. Since all ESL students want to learn a new language and to discover a culture different from their own, many selections show people meeting those goals. Second, the language of the selections was to be sufficiently understandable to allow students to be able to read them initially as a whole without interruption from text or teacher.

The selections are arranged in the text by theme and by reading difficulty, according to readability formulas. Thus, students who have read and responded to the easier selections first will be better able to handle the more difficult ones later.

Activities

The activities that follow each selection are designed to help students to clarify and interpret their initial understanding of the literature and to appreciate the effects of the language used. All activities invite the student to share clarification, interpretation, and appreciation with other students. Each teacher can organize the sharing as a class or small-group activity, in the process teaching whatever discussion skills students need.

exploring the ideas

Activities start with the section entitled "Exploring the Ideas." The exploration frequently asks students to relate the selection to their own experiences. This section also focuses on at least one—and sometimes on several—of the following aspects of literature: setting, plot, characterization, theme, author's attitude, symbol. By considering the art of a particular piece of literature, students will begin to learn how to read any piece of literature.

exploring the language

Wherever students' understanding of the literature may be enhanced by refining their initial understanding of it and by developing their appreciation of the way language is used in it, the activity section entitled "Exploring the Language" is included. To help students develop their reading ability, this section focuses on the important reading strategy of using context clues to explore the meanings of partly familiar or completely unfamiliar words. The selections were chosen because it is possible for the students to understand them as a whole the first time students read them without grasping the full meaning of each word. With such careful selection, glosses, of course, are unnecessary. However, since the selections are rich in contextual clues to the meaning of less familiar words, learning how to use those clues will not only deepen students' initial understanding of a particular piece of literature, but also will develop their ability to read any literature and their confidence that they can do so. Further, the vocabulary exercises in the activities deal with vocabulary students may wish to use in their own writing on the topics in the "Composing" section.

In addition to developing skill in using context clues to understand the meanings of words, "Exploring the Language" activities also include exercises to develop appreciation of the uses of language. Students are asked to consider the appropriateness of various aspects of language use, such as sentence structure, dialect, idiom, and social register. They are also asked to consider the effect created by strongly connotative or metaphorical language, in selections where the literature is especially rich in such language. Both kinds of consideration will not only enhance appreciation of a particular piece of literature but will also help students to learn how to appreciate all literature. The appreciation exercises, like the vocabulary exercises, can also be applied in students' own writing on the topics in the "Composing" section.

composing

The "Composing" section of the activities is a culmination of the reading process since, in order to write, students frequently will need to refer back to parts of the literature or even to reread it completely. All previous activities are designed to help students to have something to write about. In addition, the activities in "Exploring the Language" often suggest linguistic structures appropriate for their writing. Further preparation for students' writing can be found in Sandra McKay, *Fundamentals of Writing for a Specific Purpose* (Englewood Cliffs, N.J.: Prentice-Hall, 1983). The appendix of this book cross-references relevant grammatical and rhetorical exercises in *Fundamentals*.

TO THE STUDENTS

This book is an invitation to share the experiences of people who, like you, learn a new language or come to live in a culture different from the one they grew up in. We hope that the experience of reading the stories in this book will be a pleasure for you.

Reading literature in a language that is not your native one is more likely to be a pleasant experience if you first read the text through without stopping to understand the meaning of *every* word. Words only have meaning when they are used with other words. Most of the words in these stories are used in context which makes their meanings as clear as they need to be for the stories to make sense. So don't let an unfamiliar word stop you the first time you meet it; read on. There will be time later to pay attention to the word. If you stop when you see it the first time, you may lose interest in the story.

Reading these stories is rather like taking an automobile trip. Once you're on a trip, you watch for signs that tell you that you're going in the right direction. But if you stop too many times to ask for directions on the trip, you aren't likely to go very far. Instead, you put your trust in the road signs and continue. Then you can enjoy the sights you see or the feeling and ideas that occur to you at the time. Afterward, you think back over your trip, tell other people about what you noticed, discover what others may have observed, and find out about things you wondered about. If you really liked the trip, you may decide to take it again.

In the same way, when you read the stories in this book, notice what you can as you read them for the first time without stopping. Then after you've read each of them, you'll be encouraged to think about the people you've read about and to discover what other people in your class think about them. And you'll be asked to figure out the meanings of words. You'll be able to do it because there are only a few such words and because your attention will be directed to the kinds of clues that will help you. You'll also be asked to think about why a writer said that one thing is like another or about what the effect is of choosing one word rather than another.

As much fun as it is to travel, remembering it—maybe with the help of pictures—talking about it, and writing about it help you to enjoy it even more. And as involving as a story can be the first time you read it, you're sure to discover new riches in it when you reread it to explore both the ideas it has given you and the language that created the ideas. Finally, you'll be able to use your discoveries in your own writing.

Sandra McKay

Dorothy Petitt

AT THE DOOR

photo: Irene Springer.

"PROSPECTIVE IMMIGRANTS PLEASE NOTE"

Adrienne Rich

Almost everyone has had the experience of standing at a door, hesitating. What might be some reasons for such hesitation?

Either you will
go through this door
or you will not go through.

If you go through
there is always the risk
of remembering your name.

Things look at you doubly
and you must look back
and let them happen.

If you do not go through
it is possible
to live worthily

to maintain your attitudes
to hold your position
to die bravely

but much will blind you,
much will evade you,
at what cost who knows?

The door itself
makes no promises.
It is only a door.

Exploring the Ideas

Have you ever gone through a door that changed something in your life significantly? Have you ever turned away from a door? If you have, can you say why you did? Did the door itself affect your decision to enter or to turn away?

Exploring the Language

symbols

A building needs a door for people to be able to enter and leave. What building has a door for prospective immigrants to the United States, for example? Are there doors for prospective immigrants that aren't necessarily in buildings?

Is it usually risky for you to remember your name? What things, beside a means of identification, does your name stand for? How might it be risky for immigrants to remember the things their names stand for?

If someone asks you how things are, do they mean literal things? How will things change in the life of an immigrant who goes through the door? What will he or she have to do with the new things?

Do prospective immigrants have to go through the door, or do they have a choice? What will happen if they decide not to go through the door? What might be another name for the door?

Composing

describing an event

Choose one of the following topics:

TOPIC I. Do you remember an important, *real* door that you went through, such as the entrance to a new school? Describe the door itself. What were the risks you ran in going through the door? What were things like on the other side?

TOPIC II. Perhaps you have gone through a symbolic door, like deciding to come to the United States. What did you do and why? Were there risks? What were they? What were things like after you did what you did?

TOPIC III. Perhaps you decided not to go through either a real or a symbolic door. What was your decision? What were your reasons for making it? How did your life change after your decision?

photo: Fritz Henle.

photo: © 1982 Barbara Rios.

from WEST SIDE STORY

book by Arthur Laurents
music by Leonard Bernstein
lyrics by Stephen Sondheim

The play, West Side Story, *tells the story of two rival teen-age gangs in New York City. One of the gangs, called the Sharks, is Puerto Rican. In this excerpt several young immigrants from Puerto Rico are comparing life in Puerto Rico to life in the United States.*

ROSALIA: We have many pretty names at home.

ANITA: (*Mimicking*) At home, at home. If it's so nice "at home," why don't you go back there?

ROSALIA: I would like to—(*A look from* Anita)—just for a successful visit.

(*She sings nostalgically*)
Puerto Rico...
You lovely island...
Island of tropical breezes.
  Always the pineapples growing,
  Always the coffee blossoms blowing...

ANITA: (*Sings sarcastically*)
Puerto Rico...
You ugly island...
Island of tropic diseases.
  Always the hurricanes blowing,
  Always the population growing...
  And the money owing,
  And the babies crying,
  And the bullets flying.
I like the island Manhattan—
Smoke on your pipe and put that in!

ALL: (*Except* Rosalia)
I like to be in America!
O.K. by me in America!
Everything free in America
For a small fee in America!

ROSALIA:
I like the city of San Juan—

ANITA:
I know a boat you can get on.

ROSALIA:
Hundreds of flowers in full bloom—

ANITA:
Hundreds of people in each room!

ALL: (*Except* Rosalia)
Automobile in America,
Chromium steel in America,
Wire-spoke wheel in America—
Very big deal in America!

ROSALIA:
I'll drive a Buick through San Juan—

ANITA:
If there's a road you can drive on.

ROSALIA:
I'll give my cousins a free ride—

ANITA:
How you get all of them inside?

ALL: (*Except* Rosalia)
Immigrant goes to America,
Many hellos in America;
Nobody knows in America
Puerto Rico's in America.
(*The girls whistle and dance*)

ROSALIA:
When I will go back to San Juan—

ANITA:
When you will shut up and get gone!

ROSALIA:
I'll give them new washing machine—

ANITA:
What have they got there to keep clean?

ALL: (*Except* Rosalia)
I like the shores of America!
Comfort is yours in America!
Knobs on the doors in America,
Wall-to-wall floors in America!
(*They whistle and dance*)

ROSALIA:
I'll bring a TV to San Juan—

ANITA:
If there's a current to turn on.

ROSALIA:
Everyone there will give big cheer!

ANITA:
Everyone there will have moved here!
(*The song ends in a joyous dance*)

The Lights Black Out

Exploring the Ideas

the theme

Rosalia would like to return to Puerto Rico, at least for a visit. What does she see as the advantages of life in Puerto Rico? Why do you think she has to be reminded of the disadvantages?

Anita sings of the disadvantages of life in Puerto Rico. List those that she mentions. Why do you think she doesn't remember the advantages?

Why do you think everyone says that everything is free in America for a small fee? Why do you think they especially mention the automobile?

What does Anita say it will take for Rosalia to drive a Buick through San Juan? Does the picture of San Juan suggest that Anita is right?

Puerto Rico is a commonwealth of the United States. What do you think is meant by the line that nobody knows in America that Puerto Rico is in America?

The chorus sings about the comfort of life in America and says:
"Knobs on the doors in America,
Wall-to-wall floors in America!"
What do these lines suggest about life in Puerto Rico?

Exploring the Language

vocabulary

Often a reader can understand the meaning of a word by the way it is used in context. The following terms appear in the stage directions. Use the reminders of the context in which they are used to guess the meaning of the terms.

1. *mimicking*: Anita repeats what Rosalia has just said. So *mimicking* means. . . .
2. *nostalgically*: Rosalia would like to return to visit Puerto Rico. So *nostalgically* means. . . .
3. *sarcastically*: Anita, in her song, repeats the same pattern as Rosalia but sings about the negative aspects of Puerto Rico rather than the positive aspects. So *sarcastically* means. . . .

Anita and Rosalia are new immigrants to the United States; they still make errors in English. Rephrase the following lines into standard English.

1. "How you get all of them inside?"
2. "When I will go back to San Juan—"
3. "When you will shut up and get gone!"
4. "I'll give them new washing machine—"
5. "Everyone there will give big cheer!"

A common expression in English is to "put that in your pipe and smoke it," which means that someone should think about what another person has just said. How does Anita reword this idiom?

Composing

describing a place

Describe a place that you like or dislike. It can be a city, a small town, or a neighborhood. Be certain, as Rosalia and Anita have done, to describe what it is you like or dislike about this place.

photo: California Historical Society Library, Southern Pacific Photo, 1926.

THE FILIPINO AND THE DRUNKARD

William Saroyan

From William Saroyan, *The William Saroyan Reader* (New York: George Braziller Publishers, Inc., 1958).

Before the Bay Bridge was built connecting San Francisco and Oakland, California, ferries like the one pictured took people across the bay.

THIS LOUD-MOUTHED GUY IN THE BROWN CAMEL-HAIR COAT was not really mean, he was drunk. He took a sudden dislike to the small, well-dressed Filipino and began to order him around the waiting room, telling him to get back, not to crowd up among the white people. They were waiting to get on the boat and cross the bay to Oakland. If he hadn't been drunk no one would have bothered to notice him at all, but as it was, he was making a commotion in the waiting room, and while everyone seemed to be in sympathy with the Filipino, no one seemed to want to bother about coming to the boy's rescue, and the poor Filipino was becoming very frightened.

He stood among the people, and this drunkard kept pushing up against him and saying, I told you to get back. Now get back. Go away back. I fought twenty-four months in France. I'm a real American. I don't want you standing up here among white people.

The boy kept squeezing nimbly and politely out of the drunkard's way, hurrying through the crowd, not saying anything and trying his best to be as decent as possible. He kept dodging in and out, with the drunkard stumbling after him, and as time went on the drunkard's dislike grew and he began to swear at the boy. He kept saying, You fellows are the best-dressed men in San Francisco, and you make your money washing dishes. You've got no right to wear such fine clothes.

He swore a lot, and it got so bad that a lot of ladies had to imagine they were deaf and weren't hearing any of the things he was saying.

When the big door opened, the young Filipino moved swiftly among the people, fleeing from the drunkard, reaching the boat before anyone else. He ran to a corner, sat down for a moment, then got up and began looking for a more hidden place. At the other end of the boat was the drunkard. He could hear the man swearing. He looked about for a place to hide, and rushed into the lavatory. He went into one of the open compartments and bolted the door.

The drunkard entered the lavatory and began asking others in the room if they had seen the boy. He was a real American, he said. He had been wounded twice in the War.

In the lavatory he swore more freely, using words he could never use where women were present. He began to stoop and look beyond the shut doors of the various compartments. I beg your pardon, he said to those he was not seeking, and when he came to the compartment where the boy was standing, he began swearing and demanding that the boy come out.

You can't get away from me, he said. You got no right to use a place white men use. Come out or I'll break the door.

Go away, the boy said.

The drunkard began to pound on the door.

You got to come out sometime, he said. I'll wait here till you do.

Go away, said the boy. I've done nothing to you.

He wondered why none of the men in the lavatory had the decency to calm the drunkard and take him away, and then he realized there were no other men in the lavatory.

Go away, he said.

The drunkard answered with curses, pounding the door.

Behind the door, the boy's bitterness grew to rage. He began to tremble, not fearing the man but fearing the rage growing in himself. He brought the knife from his pocket and drew open the sharp blade, holding the knife in his fist so tightly that the nails of his fingers cut into the flesh of his palm.

Go away, he said. I have a knife. I do not want any trouble.

The drunkard said he was an American. Twenty-four months in France. Wounded twice. Once in the leg, and once in the thigh. He would not go away. He was afraid of no dirty little yellow-belly Filipino with a knife. Let the Filipino come out, he was an American.

I will kill you, said the boy. I do not want to kill any man. You are drunk. Go away.

Please do not make any trouble, he said earnestly.

He could hear the motor of the boat pounding. It was like his rage pounding. It was a feeling of having been humiliated, chased about and made to hide, and now it was a wish to be free, even if he had to kill. He threw the door open and tried to rush beyond the man, the knife tight in his fist, but the drunkard caught him by the sleeve and drew him back. The sleeve of the boy's coat ripped, and the boy turned and thrust the knife into the side of the drunkard, feeling it scrape against rib bone. The drunkard shouted and screamed at once, then caught the boy at the throat, and the boy thrust the knife into the side of the man many times, as a boxer jabs in the clinches.

When the drunkard could no longer hold him and had fallen to the floor, the boy rushed from the room, the knife still in his hand, blood dripping from the blade, his hat gone, his hair mussed, and the sleeve of his coat badly torn.

Everyone knew what he had done, yet no one moved.

The boy ran to the front of the boat, seeking some place to go, then ran back to a corner, no one daring to speak to him, and everyone aware of his crime.

There was no place to go, and before the officers of the boat arrived he stopped suddenly and began to shout at the people.

I did not want to hurt him, he said. Why didn't you stop him? Is it right to chase a man like a rat? You knew he was drunk. I did not want to hurt him, but he would not let me go. He tore my coat and tried to choke me. I told him I would kill him if he would not go away. It is not my fault. I must go to Oakland to see my brother. He is sick. Do you think I am looking for trouble when my brother is sick? Why didn't you stop him?

Exploring the Ideas

the characters

After reading the story, you very likely have formed an opinion about the Filipino, the drunkard and the crowd. From the following list, choose those adjectives that you think best describe the Filipino. Which best describe the drunkard? Which best describe the crowd? (Some of them may in your opinion describe more than one of them.) Add to the list any other adjectives that you feel describe the characters.

aggressive	frightened	innocent	rude
apathetic	guilty	polite	shy
cowardly	honest	prejudiced	violent
decent	impulsive	proud	other

The following list describes specific things that the characters did. For each one, give an adjective that characterizes this behavior. You may use the adjectives listed above or others. In many cases, more than one adjective may be appropriate.

Example

The drunkard kept pushing up against the Filipino and telling him to get back.
Characteristics: aggressive, rude.

1. The drunkard said several times that he had fought in the war and that he was a real American.
2. The drunkard swore at the boy.
3. The Filipino ran to a corner of the boat and looked for a place to hide.
4. The Filipino said that he had a knife and that he did not want any trouble.
5. The Filipino opened the compartment door and tried to rush beyond the drunkard.
6. The drunkard caught the boy by the sleeve and threw him back.
7. The Filipino thrust the knife into the side of the drunkard.
8. No one dared to speak to the Filipino.

author's attitude

Authors have several indirect ways they can tell their readers how they feel about the characters and events in their stories. Their aims in writing stories are to persuade you to feel as they do, but they don't want to argue with you directly. Saroyan uses two of these indirect ways in "The Filipino and the Drunkard."

First, Saroyan shows his opinion of his two main characters by the terms he uses to introduce them. How does Saroyan introduce the drunkard? How does he describe the Filipino? What do the terms suggest about Saroyan's attitude toward the two characters?

Second, Saroyan twice tells you directly what one of the characters is thinking and feeling, but not the other character. Which one? Why do you suppose he chose that character rather than the other one? What effect do the descriptions of the character's thoughts and feelings create?

the theme

Indicate if you agree or disagree with each of the following comments.

1. The Filipino could not understand why the passengers didn't calm the drunkard down. What do you think about the passengers' behavior?
   - They acted properly by not getting involved in someone else's business.
   - They should have reported the matter to the boat officials and allowed them to deal with the matter.
   - They should have verbally warned the drunkard to leave the Filipino alone.

- They should have physically restrained the drunkard.

2. The passengers did not get involved because:
   - They were afraid that the drunkard would beat them up.
   - They felt that it was the job of the police to deal with the problem.
   - They were afraid they would have to spend time in court if the drunkard got arrested.
   - They thought that the incident wasn't very important and that the Filipino could handle it himself.
3. The Filipino:
   - Did everything he could to avoid a physical conflict with the drunkard.
   - Should have yelled for help until the boat officials came.
   - Should have stayed in the compartment until the man went away or until they reached Oakland.
   - Should not have gotten on the boat.

Have you ever read of a case in the United States or another country when a crowd witnessed a violent crime and did nothing to stop it? Do you think this is more likely to happen in a large or small community? Why?

Obviously the drunkard thinks that he is a "real American" for he insists upon it several times in the story.

- Do you feel that the man was a "real American"?
- Did the other passengers think that the man was a "real American"?
- Does Saroyan think that the man was a "real American"?
- Do you think that the Filipino was a "real American"?
- Do you think that the other passengers on the boat were "real Americans"?

Imagine that the Filipino has been brought to court for stabbing the drunkard. The lawyer for the Filipino and the lawyer for the prosecution look through the list of facts below. Organize these facts into four groups: those that the Filipino's lawyer could use in court, those that the prosecution could use in court, those that both sides might use in court, and those that neither side would use.

1. The Filipino had a knife.
2. The man was drunk.
3. The Filipino was obviously doing his best to avoid the drunkard.
4. The Filipino was "small."

5. The drunkard fought twenty-four months in France.
6. The drunkard was swearing at the boy.
7. The Filipino was well-dressed.
8. The Filipino's sleeve was badly torn, his hat was gone, and his hair was mussed.
9. The Filipino shouted at the people, asking them why they had not helped him.
10. The Filipino's brother was sick.
11. The Filipino stabbed the drunkard several times.
12. The drunkard had been wounded twice in the war.
13. The drunkard looked beneath the shut doors of various compartments, apologizing to those he was not seeking.
14. The drunkard kept pushing up against the Filipino.
15. When the doors opened, the Filipino fled from the man and looked for a hidden place on the boat.
16. The Filipino locked himself in a compartment in the lavatory.
17. The drunkard yelled, "Come out or I'll break the door."
18. The drunkard shouted that he would wait until the Filipino came out.

Assume that you are a member of the jury at the trial of the Filipino. The judge has instructed you as follows:

- First, if you find that the Filipino did not do what he is accused of doing or that he acted in self-defense, then you must find him not guilty. Self-defense means that the Filipino used a reasonable amount of force to protect himself from the drunkard after having made every reasonable effort to escape.
- Second, if you find that the Filipino planned in advance to kill the drunkard, then you must find him guilty of first-degree, premeditated murder.
- Third, if you find that the Filipino intended to kill the drunkard but decided to do so on the spur of the moment or in intense anger, then you must find him guilty of second-degree murder.
- Fourth, if you find that the Filipino did not intend to kill the drunkard but only to hurt the drunkard, then you must find him guilty of third-degree murder or voluntary manslaughter.
- Finally, if you find that the Filipino did not intend to kill or hurt the drunkard but took action that might be expected to injure him, then you must find him guilty of involuntary manslaughter.

As a member of the jury, decide which of these categories should apply to the Filipino. Then give your verdict to the judge.

Exploring the Language

descriptive language

Many of the words in the passage were selected by Saroyan to precisely describe the action of the story. For example, Saroyan writes that the young Filipino *rushed* into the lavatory. Use the following reminders of situations in the story and the reminders about common experiences to guess the meaning of the descriptive words in italics.

1. "The boy kept *squeezing nimbly* and politely out of the dunkard's way, hurrying through the crowd. . . ." (line 15)
   There are many people in a crowd. So *squeezing* probably means. . . .
   The boy is able to get through the crowd. So *nimbly* probably means. . . .
2. "He kept *dodging* in and out, with the drunkard *stumbling* after him. . . ." (line 17)
   The boy had to go around many people to get away. So *dodging* probably means. . . .
   How does a drunkard walk? So *stumbling* probably means. . . .
3. ". . . .the young Filipino moved swiftly among the people, *fleeing* from the drunkard, ..." (line 26)
   What was the boy trying to do? So *fleeing* probably means. . . .
4. The drunkard "began to *stoop* and look beyond the shut doors of the various compartments." (line 37)
   What are doors like in a lavoratory? The door was shut. So *stoop* probably means. . . .
5. ". . . .the boy turned and *thrust* the knife into the side of the drunkard, ..." (line 70)
   He then felt the knife scrape against the rib bone. So *thrust* probably means. . . .

using quotations

Saroyan includes several statements made by the Filipino and the drunkard. Even though they are direct quotations, he has chosen not to put them in quotation marks. For example, near the end of the story he includes a statement made by the Filipino: Go away, he said. Find other sentences in the text which are direct quotations. Why do you think Saroyan has not used quotation marks?

Composing

describing a personality

Write a brief essay in which you characterize the Filipino or the drunkard in "The Filipino and the Drunkard." Select one adjective that you feel best describes the character. Then cite specific details from the story that demonstrate that they are this type of person. Be sure to include only the facts that illustrate the particular characteristic that you have chosen. Thus, if you choose to describe the Filipino as polite, or the drunkard as patriotic, or either one as guilty or innocent, include only the details in the story that support this characteristic.

photo: courtesy of Jade Snow Wong.

"A MEASURE OF FREEDOM"

Jade Snow Wong

From pp. 121–124 in *Fifth Chinese Daughter* by Jade Snow Wong.

Jade Snow Wong grew up in San Francisco's Chinatown, the fifth daughter of Chinese immigrants who ran an overall factory, although in China her father had been a scholar. In writing her autobiography, she observed the Chinese custom of referring to herself by her name, rather than using "I."

So, WITHOUT MUCH ENTHUSIASM, JADE SNOW decided upon junior college. Now it was necessary to inform mama and daddy. She chose an evening when the family was at dinner. All of them were in their customary places, and daddy, typically, was in conversation with Older Brother about the factory:

"Blessing, when do you think Lot Number fifty-one twenty-six will be finished? I want to ask for a check from our jobber so that I can have enough cash for next week's payroll."

To which Older Brother replied, "As soon as mama is through with the seams in Mrs. Lee's and Mrs. Choy's bundles, the women can finish the hems. Another day, probably."

Mama had not been consulted: therefore, she made no comment. Silence descended as the Wongs continued their meal, observing the well-learned precept that talk was not permissible while eating.

Jade Snow considered whether to break the silence. Three times she thought over what she had to say, and still found it worth saying. This also was according to family precept.

"Daddy," she said, "I have made up my mind to enter junior college here in San Francisco. I will find a steady job to pay my expenses, and by working in the summers I'll try to save enough money to take me through my last two years at the university."

Then she waited. Everyone went on eating. No one said a word. Apparently no one was interested enough to be curious. But at least no one objected. It was settled.

Junior college was at first disappointing in more ways than one. There was none of the glamor usually associated with college because the institution was so young that it had not yet acquired buildings of its own. Classes were held all over the city, wherever accommodations were available. The first days were very confusing to Jade Snow, especially when she discovered that she must immediately decide upon a college major.

While waiting to register, she thumbed through the catalogue in search of a clue. English . . . mathematics . . . chemistry. . . . In the last semester of high school she had found chemistry particularly fascinating; so with a feeling of assurance she wrote that as her major on the necessary forms and went to a sign-up table.

"I wish to take the lecture and laboratory classes for Chemistry 1A," she informed the gray-haired man who presided there.

He looked at her, a trifle impatiently, she thought.

"Why?"

"Because I like it." To herself she sounded reasonable.

"But you are no longer in high school. Chemistry here is a difficult subject on a university level, planned for those who are majoring in medicine, engineering, or the serious sciences."

Jade Snow set her chin stubbornly. "I still want to take Chemistry 1A."

Sharply he questioned: "What courses in mathematics have you had? What were your grades?"

Finally Jade Snow's annoyance rose to the surface. "Straight A's. But why must you ask? Do you think I would want to take a course I couldn't pass? Why don't you sign me up and let the instructor be the judge of my ability?"

"Very well," he replied stiffly. "I'll accept you in the class. And for your information, young lady, I am the instructor!"

With this inauspicious start, Jade Snow began her college career.

To take care of finances, she now needed to look for work. Through a friend she learned that a Mrs. Simpson needed someone to help with household work. "Can you cook?" was Mrs. Simpson's first question.

Jade Snow considered a moment before answering. Certainly she could cook Chinese food, and she remembered a common Chinese saying, "A Chinese can cook foreign food as well as, if not better than, the foreigners, but a foreigner cannot cook Chinese food fit for the Chinese." On this reasoning it seemed safe to say "Yes."

After some further discussion Jade Snow was hired. Cooking, she discovered, included everything from pastries, puddings, meats, steaks, and vegetables, to sandwiches. In addition, she served the meals, washed dishes, kept the house clean, did the light laundry and ironing for Mr. and Mrs. Simpson and their career daughter—and always appeared in uniform, which she thoroughly disliked. In return she received twenty dollars a month. At night, she did her studying at home, and sometimes after a hard day she was so tired that the walk from the Simpson flat to the streetcar on Chestnut Street was a blessed respite, a time to relax and admire the moon if she could find it, and to gather fresh energy for whatever lay ahead.

Desserts, quite ignored in a Chinese household, were of first importance in the Simpson household. One particular Saturday, Jade

Snow was told to bake a special meringue sponge cake with a fancy fruit filling of whipped cream and peeled and seeded grapes. Following a very special recipe of Mrs. Simpson's, she mixed it for the first time and preheated the oven. Mrs. Simpson came into the kitchen, checked and approved the prepared cake batter, and said that she would judge when it was done. Meantime she and her husband and their guests lounged happily in the garden.

Almost an hour passed. The meringue was baking in a slow oven. The recipe said not to open the door, as the cake might fall. An hour and a quarter passed, and the pastry smelled sweetly delicate. Yet Mrs. Simpson did not come. Jade Snow wondered whether or not to call her. But she remembered that her employer disliked being disturbed when entertaining officials of her husband's company.

After an hour and forty-five minutes the cake no longer smelled delicate. Jade Snow was worn out! What could she do? At last, there was a rush of high-heeled footsteps; swish went the kitchen door, and Mrs. Simpson burst in, flushed from the sun or excitement.

"I must look at that meringue cake," she burst out.

The oven door was pulled open, and Jade Snow peered in anxiously over her employer's shoulder. Too late! It had fallen and become a tough, brown mass. Jade Snow was dumb with a crushed heart, inspecting the flattened pancake, mentally reviewing all the processes of whipping, measuring, and sifting that she had gone through for hours to achieve this unpalatable result.

Mrs. Simpson crisply broke through to her anguish "Well, there's nothing to be done but for you to make another."

That afternoon was a torturous nightmare and a fever of activity—to manage another meringue cake, to get rolls mixed, salad greens cleaned and crisped, vegetables cut, meat broiled, the table set, and all of the other details of a "company" dinner attended to. By the time she was at last washing the dishes and tidying the dining room, she felt strangely vague. She hadn't taken time to eat her dinner; she was too tired anyway. How she wished that she had been asked to cook a Chinese dinner instead of this interminable American meal, especially that cake!

Exploring the Ideas

the theme

This brief excerpt from *Fifth Chinese Daughter* illustrates several customs of Chinese culture as well as American culture. For each of the following passages describe what seems to be the convention of the Wong family that is stated or implied. Then indicate if this convention is followed by your family and if not, describe what is the usual custom for a similar situation in your home.

Example

"She chose an evening when the family was at dinner. All of them were in their customary places. . . ."
Wong's convention: Each member of the family usually sits in the same place at the table.
Your family: People in my family usually sit at different places.

1. "So, without much enthusiasm, Jade Snow decided upon junior college. Now it was necessary to inform mama and daddy."
2. "Silence descended as the Wongs continued their meal, observing the well-learned precept that talk was not permissible while eating."
3. "Jade Snow considered whether to break the silence. Three times she thought over what she had to say, and still found it worth saying. This also was according to family precept."
4. "I will find a steady job to pay my expenses, and by working in the summers I'll try to save enough money to take me through my last two years at the university."
5. "Then she waited. Everyone went on eating. No one said a word. . . . But at least no one objected. It was settled."

For each of the following passages describe what is the stated or implied convention of the Simpson family. Then indicate if this convention is the same for your family.

1. "Desserts, quite ignored in a Chinese household, were of first importance in the Simpson household."
2. "Jade Snow wondered whether or not to call her [Mrs. Simpson]. But she remembered that her employer disliked being disturbed when entertaining officials of her husband's company."

If you had been Jade Snow what would you have done about the cake?

author's attitude

Jade Snow Wong comments at times on how she felt, always talking about herself in the third person as if she were someone else. For example, in describing the beginning of her college career she writes, "The first days were very confusing to Jade Snow." List other passages that describe her feelings. Why do you think she preferred to talk about her feelings in the third person?

Exploring the Language

vocabulary

Use the reminders of what happened in the story, and the information on common word parts to guess the meaning of the words in italics.

1. "With this *inauspicious* start, Jade Snow began her college career." (line 55)
   In is a common prefix that means not. The man who questions her choice of major turns out to be her chemistry teacher. So inauspicious probably means. . . .
2. ". . . sometimes after a hard day she was so tired that the walk from the Simpson flat to the streetcar on Chestnut Street was a blessed *respite*, a time to relax and admire the moon if she could find it, and to gather fresh energy for whatever lay ahead." (line 73)
   The walk to the streetcar was a time to relax. So a *respite* is a. . . .
3. "How she wished that she had been asked to cook a Chinese dinner instead of this *interminable* American meal, especially that cake!" (line 111)
   Remember that *in* means not. The root of the word is *terminate* which means to bring to an end. The American meal which included salad, a main course and dessert must have been. . . .

photo: Sandra Weiner.

"DORIA RAMIREZ"

Sandra Weiner

Sandra Weiner, a photographer, interviewed several Chicano migrant workers and their families to write a book about them. The various chapters in her book are based on taped conversations with the characters. Doria Ramirez is, of course, a nonnative speaker of English. Although she makes errors in English, she is able to vividly describe her feelings about being a migrant worker.

I AM DORIA RAMIREZ AND I AM EIGHTEEN YEARS OLD. I went to school when I was ten years and got out when I was thirteen because I had to help my parents. We used to get up at 3:30 in the morning to pick potatoes and I didn't like it. Always I didn't like it. It was very cold. Another reason I had to leave—I didn't have any shoes with me and I didn't have any sweater and it was in the winter time.

I knew we didn't have any money so I couldn't say, "Poppa I need shoes for my feet." But when I saw all the other children with shoes I knew that there had to be a way to change that life. The way I was feeling I didn't want my sisters to feel the same thing. It was then I started thinking that this was not a life for the migrant worker or any worker. Without shoes and warm clothes all these Mexican children could not go to school. My father did not feel it this way but when I used to see my younger brothers working so hard and feeling so tired at age thirteen years, I wanted to see them in a different position in their life.

We are nine in our family and we were being paid piece rate. With a big family you can work a long day and think you are making some money. But in the winter time when there is no work it doesn't help to have such a large family. My father would never go to the Welfare. He always told us that he didn't like to go to the Welfare because you had to let the Governor's office know what size shoe he was wearing and what size underwear—and he didn't like it. It was too private. My mother tried to sew our clothes but when you don't have any money you have the time, but you can't buy the material to sew.

The growers give us the jobs because we are a large family. I am not afraid to ask the growers for more money because I used to see families just starving. My father asked, "Why do you always have to argue with the grower?" But always in a family there has to be one member that asks. There has to be one that talks too much. And I was the one. My father would say, "Don't ask for more or they will not let us work and take all the money away." To him it always has to be the way they gave us. I said, "No, that's not enough, I don't want to live that way." He would answer, "My father lived that way and we can live the same way."

We do whatever each farm needs, either thinning, or tying, or hoeing, or picking. We have picked almost every fruit and vegetable growing, but the hardest job that I know, as a woman, is sugarbeets. Even the men say it is hard. After thinning you leave each plant five inches apart from the other. That's very hard because always you have to be bent over on your knees with a small hoe, maybe twelve hours and this makes you sick with the kidneys or back. You must thin it while it is still a young plant. If you try sitting it doesn't work and you do not get the work done.

There was this man, he was a labor contractor for the ranchers, and he hired about 200 people and I made about 33 or 32 rows that day. You have to be a fast person. I had gone with shoes and socks into the field but I came out without the shoes or socks because the blisters on my feet they were paining me. So I went back to the car to lie down because I couldn't stand or move. I was already half with fever from tiredness. The labor contractor didn't want to pay my father and he was saying, "Well, your daughter has to come out and get the money, she knows how to sign her name." And even though I was feeling so sick I was happy because I thought we were going to have so much money for the family. And all we got was seven dollars for nine people working twelve hours.

I always had to work to help my parents because I love my parents. We just stick together. This is why it's good to have a big family because together we make our own home. A small home but it's my home and I don't need any other home because I have my family. We have two rooms, a kitchen and another room, and we sleep like hot dogs.

I get up when my mother starts preparing the lunches for the day in the field. She bakes bread and makes tacos and tortillas. At night when we return home she washes the clothes and hangs up just pants on the clothes wire, and the neighbors say, "You have only boys," and my mother said, "No, we are six girls and three boys." In the evenings parents are tired and do not talk very much.

Another time I saw my father crying. That day had been a bad day for us. We had arrived in the field at 4:30 in the morning and they had to put big lights on the tractors so we could see how to pick the potatoes. And we picked all day until 5 o'clock in the evening. There were six of us and we earned only twelve dollars. And that was when my father wanted to cry. It was then I started to think again that I must make a change. My father, he said, "Now I understand you and why you are so angry at the growers."

Once I got really mad when I was working with one of the growers and we were organizing and he fired all the people that were organizing or interested in a union. When we walked from the fields everybody walked with us. But the next day the farmer found other people to work for him and we knew it would take a long time before all the migrant workers understood about the union. It took my father a long time. Now I spend a lot of time helping to organize farm workers and we hope the dream of a union will come true. It's just like Martin Luther King when he said, "I have a dream too."

I am much happier now because I am learning so much. When I was in school I didn't learn anything. I had to rush from school to pick cotton and I would forget the English and arithmetic. I never learned to speak English but I learned English real good when I started walking on the picket lines asking people not to buy grapes in the stores that sold them. At the first boycott they wouldn't take me because I didn't speak the language. So I had to learn fast to speak English. Everybody helped me who knew how to speak it. I still don't know how to read or write but I will learn.

It is hard to believe now that I had lived the way we did for so long. I remember at home on Saturday we would all take baths and eat together and then my father would play the trumpet. My sister and my brother-in-law played the guitar and my little sister played the guitar and we would sing and dance. Even though our life is with so much work we love to have fun and have some happiness. You have to carry some happiness in your heart.

Exploring the Ideas

the plot

The following statements describe various aspects of Doria's life. Indicate which statements you consider to be accurate and which statements you consider inaccurate. Correct the inaccurate ones.

1. She went to school for five years.
2. One reason she left school was because she didn't have any shoes or sweater.
3. There were nine children in her family.
4. Because they had such a large family, they were able to earn all the money they needed.
5. Her father didn't want to go on welfare.
6. Doria was afraid to ask the growers for more money.
7. The family picked only sugarbeets.

8. Sugarbeets were difficult to thin because they had to be thinned while kneeling.
9. The family had nine boys.
10. Doria learned to speak English in school.

themes

Why did her father not want to go on welfare? Do you think he should have gone on welfare? What excuse does her father give for not wanting to ask the growers for more money? What excuse does he give for continuing to live the way they do? What kind of a man do you think he is? What makes you think so?

What two incidents does Doria describe which show how unfair their wages are? Why do you think the growers fired all the people who were trying to organize a union? What made Doria want to learn English?

photo: Stephen Kelley.

"WYOMING BEGINNINGS"

Beltran Paris as told to William A. Douglass

From *Beltran: Basque Sheepman of the American West*, by Beltran Paris as told to William A. Douglass.

Beltran Paris was born in 1888 in French Basque country and at twenty-three left France to work with his cousin as a sheepherder in Gillette, Wyoming. In 1967, William A. Douglass met Beltran and, based on his conversations with him, wrote an account of his life.

WHEN WE GOT TO GILLETTE I expected to see my cousins waiting for me, or at least somebody. Maybe the sheep foreman was going to be there, he was a Basque from the town of Banca. I wrote my cousins before leaving France so they knew I was coming, but nobody was there. I waited and waited and nobody came.

I couldn't stay there like that. I had the address of one hotel in Gillette and I saw their sign from the station. The owner was a woman and I began to talk to her in French but she didn't understand. I was surprised. I knew that in the United States nobody was going to understand Basque but I thought pretty near everyone would know some French. Anyway, she was a nice lady. I gave her the address of the ranch and I could see she knew about that place. Every few days somebody came from there to Gillette with horses and a wagon to get grub. I couldn't understand her words but I could tell I had to stay in the hotel until somebody came for me.

So I started waiting, but then I got hungrier and hungrier. I had those forty American dollars in my pocket but I didn't know how to buy anything. Finally, I just had to try so I went outside. I saw a sign which said "restaurant." Well I knew what that was because we have the same word in French. I thought maybe it was a French place, but when I went there it was Chinese. I went into the kitchen and started talking and the Chinaman that was cooking gave me a glass of water. I said, "No, no, no!" and he started laughing.

Then he knew what I wanted and took me into the dining room. There was a woman working there and she gave me a menu. I couldn't understand it so I just asked her to bring me anything at all to eat. I'll never forget that. She brought me pork chops and they were awfully good. I ate everything but then I didn't know how much I owed. I took out my money and just held it out. She took a bill and brought me back lots of silver. I knew then that I had plenty of money.

I left and went back to the hotel but in about two hours that meal wasn't enough. I was feeling hungry so I went to the restaurant again. The waitress knew me and didn't bring the menu. She just brought whatever she thought was best.

I stayed that way for four days before the teamster came to town. Then the lady who owned the hotel told me to get ready because I had to go. There were three big wagons and eight horses. She told me to put my suitcases in there. She didn't ask me for any money, maybe she thought the boss was going to pay the hotel bill. But I paid her and climbed up on the lead wagon. The teamster shouted "giyyap" and we started out.

It was fifty miles to the ranch. After a while we stopped for lunch. He built a fire and we had some canned food to eat. We couldn't talk at all but he handed me a coffee pot and I knew he wanted some water. I started walking and went over a hill, but I couldn't find any springs or creeks. Then I saw a lake and went over there. Well it was terrible water. There was cow manure floating all over it, just like a bunch of birds. So I kept looking for a spring but I couldn't find one. Finally I was worried. I was taking lots of time and I was ashamed to go back without any water. I thought I must have missed the spring. So I just moved the manure away a little bit and took some of the lake water. It was awfully dirty.

When I got back he started talking and I knew he was saying that I took a long time. Then he made some coffee. Well in my country it was a special treat to drink coffee. We couldn't afford it. I liked coffee and whenever I had the chance I would drink two or three cups. But not out there. He handed me some and I said, "No, no coffee!" He thought maybe I was sick or something and then he tried again. Well I was thinking of that cow manure and I just couldn't drink it. Anyway, he drank three cups and then we had to go.

It took us three days to get to the ranch. It wasn't much of a place. There was one old guy alone there and he wasn't Basque, so I couldn't talk to him either. The sheepherders were ten or fifteen miles away. We unloaded the wagons and then that teamster left me right there with the old man. He had a little house and he just kept care of four or five horses. They didn't even have a milk cow.

There were sheep corrals all around the house and I saw hundreds of sheepskins drying on the fences. I didn't know what to think. I wondered if this was a slaughterhouse. Then I got worried; I thought maybe they were going to ask me to butcher sheep and I didn't want that kind of work. I said to myself, "I gonna ask for a herding job."

Later I found out that it had been a real bad winter and they lost lots of sheep. When my cousins wrote me the boss had twenty thousand sheep and maybe five or six herders. Well that winter they lost about half, maybe ten thousand. Some of the sheep froze to death and others starved. They skinned as many as they could just to save something.

Anyway, I didn't know what to do next. I was there with that guy but we couldn't understand each other and there was no work to do either. I just walked around a little bit and I stayed like that for three days.

Finally, the sheep foreman from Banca came and I sure was glad. He said he was taking me to my cousin's sheep camp. When we got close I could hear the sheep coming and there was a man, too. He started walking towards me. It was early springtime and still cold and he was wearing a heavy sheepskin jacket. It had a big collar turned up on his neck and he had a cap with earflaps pulled way down over his head. In that country sometimes it gets fifty below zero in the winter and nobody shaves. His face was all black, just as black as a Negro, and I couldn't recognize him. Then he started laughing and talking and I could see that it was my cousin, Joseph Curutchet.

They told me that I was going to stay there with Joe and help him out. All the sheep already had herders until lambing so they didn't need me. That way I could learn about herding, too. We lived together there in a sheep wagon and slept in the same bed.

There was no snow left in that place but everything was muddy. There wasn't any feed yet and those sheep were real weak. Joe said every day more were dying. Sometimes one would get stuck in the mud and I would run over and pull it out. In the Old Country you did everything to save one animal, but here it was different. Joe just said, "Bah, leave it alone; it's gonna die anyway." After that winter he didn't care and he was used to that, but I just couldn't do it. I had to help the sheep somehow.

After about a week the ground began to dry out and a little grass started growing. By gosh in about fifteen days the country was all green and we had pretty good feed. The sheep were getting stronger all the time. Then we knew they were going to make it and we saved all the rest.

Close by there was a big river. I don't know where it came from, maybe hundreds of miles away. It was about a hundred feet wide. In summer it dried up but in the spring even a saddle horse couldn't cross it. Joe told me that my cousin Jean Curutchet was herding on the other side. I could barely make out his sheep, they were so far away. Well one morning I saw him coming to the river. He knew from the camptender that I was with Joe and that's why he was coming. When I saw that I started running. In those days I could run ten miles easy, so I ran down to that river. I knew I couldn't cross but I was hoping we could talk from one side to the other. I waved at him and started hollering but I couldn't hear anything. The water was too noisy. He had a face just like Joe's, all black. Anyway, we stayed that way a long time just looking at each other. Then I went back to camp and didn't see Jean again until lambing.

Exploring the Ideas

the characters

When Beltran Paris arrived in Gillette, he faced several difficult situations. For each situation, describe how Beltran dealt with the problem.

Example

Problem: Beltran wanted someone he knew to meet him in Gillette.
Beltran's solution: He wrote to his cousins before leaving France so that they knew he was coming.

1. No one was at the station to meet him.
2. He was hungry but no one spoke French.
3. He couldn't understand the menu.
4. He didn't know how much he owed for the meal.
5. He couldn't find a spring or creek to get water for coffee.
6. He didn't want to drink the coffee.
7. When he got to the ranch, the old man didn't speak English.
8. He wanted to talk to his cousin, Jean, on the other side of the river.

List several adjectives that could be used to describe the manner in which Beltran Paris dealt with these problems.

the theme

Beltran Paris mentions that in Basque country everything was done to save one animal. What did they do in Wyoming? How did Beltran feel about this?

Exploring the Language

spoken english

This account of Beltran's life is based on his taped conversations with William A. Douglass. Thus, some elements of the style of the text reflect spoken English. For example, many short sentences are combined with *and*, and *but*, which is typical of spoken English. In describing the hotel owner, Beltran states that "The owner was a woman *and* I began to talk to her in French *but* she didn't understand." Find other examples of such sentences in the text.

In addition, the text contains several expressions that are typical of spoken English such as *anyway, well, then, finally,* and *by gosh.* List sentences from the text that include these expressions.

The selection from *Small Hands, Big Hands* is also based on taped conversations. In both instances, the main characters related their life history to a third person. In the case of Doria Ramirez, Sandra Weiner did very little editing of the conversation. Why do you think she didn't edit? Do you think Beltran's editor has changed his taped conversation? If you do think he did, what do you think the changes were?

Both authors chose to tell the story in the first person, "I." Why do you think they made that choice?

Composing

describing an event

Choose one of the following topics:

TOPIC I. Select an event that you remember quite well. It can be one from your childhood or a more recent event. As Jade Snow Wong has done, describe both the event and how you felt. Of course, your description, unlike Jade Snow Wong's, should be in the first person.

TOPIC II. Doria Ramirez describes two specific times when she was not paid an adequate amount for her work. The fact that she rarely received a just wage convinced her to join the union. Ultimately, it was her activity in the union that helped her to learn English. Describe a specific event that you feel motivated you to want to learn English.

TOPIC III. Beltran Paris was faced with several difficult situations when he arrived at Gillette, Wyoming. Yet through ingenuity he found a way to deal with each situation. Describe a difficult experience that you have had and how you dealt with it. As Paris has done, you might describe a problem that arose because no one spoke your native language.

photo: Ezra Stoller, Esto, Windows on the World.

from SWEET PROMISED LAND

Robert Laxalt

From pp. 61–64 in *Sweet Promised Land* by Robert Laxalt. Copyright

Robert Laxalt's father, Dominique, came to America when he was sixteen. In the opening passage of Sweet Promised Land, *Laxalt describes his father as follows:*

> *My father was a sheepherder, and his home was the hills. So it began when he was a boy in the misted Pyrenees of France, and so it was to be for the most of his lifetime in the lonely Sierra of Nevada. And seeing him in a moment's pause on some high ridge, with the wind tearing at his wild thickness of iron-gray hair and flattening his clothes to his lean frame, you could understand why this was what he was meant to be.*

The following excerpt describes his father at the age of sixty-three stopping in New York City on the way back to his homeland for the first time since he came to America.

NOTHING HE COULD HAVE WORN WOULD HAVE MADE ANY DIFFERENCE. He was as out of place in this New York café as the tuxedoed waiter would have been in a dusty horse corral. In this dimly lighted gathering of well-groomed people with soft faces and hands, he was an oddity with a leathered and creased face and hands that looked more like darkened wood than flesh.

As we entered the café and followed the headwaiter to the table, people turned and watched. Some regarded him with curious expressions, and a few with a resentment for which they could probably not find words. There was one, a pretty and tailored lady just beginning to gray, whose eyes softened, as if she could remember an old country father with a graven face, who had been a workingman too.

And yet, in spite of this scrutiny, my father was not ill at ease. Instead, he was as interested in the people about him as they were in him. He sat there as quietly and detachedly as if he were in a darkened movie house, observing everything and everyone in the café. His expression was as rapt as a child's, and he was having just as much fun.

The waiters seemed to intrigue him the most. His eyes followed them relentlessly as they moved about, taking in their stiff shirt fronts and black ties and short jackets, and, mostly, the stiff correctness of their manner.

It was inevitable that my father's first altercation would be with a waiter. The warning came when we ordered a drink before dinner, and my father asked for a little glass of claret. He held up his thumb and forefinger to designate that he wanted "a short one." The waiter looked twice, and then smiled in understanding.

We made it through the soup and the salad without incident. It began when the waiter came to take away our salad plates and put on others for the main course. He collected John's and mine, and then reached for my father's. But he could not lift it, because my father was holding it to the table with both hands.

"I'm sorry," said the waiter. "I thought you were finished."

"I am finished," said my father.

"Oh," said the waiter, and again reached for the salad plate. My father held on.

"May I take your plate, sir?" said the waiter.

"No," said my father mildly.

The waiter stood in confused silence for a moment. "But I have to put another plate there, sir."

My father shook his head. "It's all right," he said. "Don't go to any bother."

The waiter blinked, and then smiled weakly. "Oh, it's no bother at all," he said, and again reached for the plate.

This time, my father put his hands over the plate to protect it. The waiter stopped short and straightened up. He looked at us in something akin to frenzy, and John gestured with his head. The waiter retreated to the back of the room and stood there watching us from long distance. He was pale and he still had a plate in his hands.

"Pop," said John. "Why don't you give him your plate?"

My father shrugged. "It's clean enough," he said.

This time John blinked. "I don't understand what you mean."

"They shouldn't waste a plate," said my father. "This one's fine."

John regarded my father for a long moment. "It's really no bother," he said. "They've got a washer back there that does all the work."

"Well, they might run short," my father said.

"I'm telling you, Pop," said John. "There's no danger." He took a deep drag of his cigarette and leaned forward again. "Pop," he said. "You're going to get that waiter in trouble."

"What?" said my father concernedly.

"It's this way," said John. "They're supposed to put a new plate on for each course. That's the way the management wants it. If the waiter doesn't do it and one of the managers sees him, he gets fired on the spot."

"I never heard of such a thing," my father said.

"It's true," said John. "That waiter's probably worried plenty by now."

"Well, hell," said my father. "Tell him to take it then."

John signaled for the waiter and he came forward. When John nodded his head that it was all right, he reached out gingerly and took the salad plate. "I'm sorry, poor fellow," said my father. "I didn't know you was that close to losing your job."

"Oh, that's all right," said the waiter, comprehending nothing at this stage.

After that, he seemed to expect anything. When dinner was done, my father helped him clear the crumbs from the table by gathering his own into his cupped hand. The waiter merely held out his hand to receive them. When my father was through dropping them in, the waiter said, "Thank you."

And later, when he brought us the check, he stood by with inscrutable countenance as my father pulled his passport and wallet bundle out of his pocket, set it on the table, unwound the black inner-tube band, untied the string, and gave him the money. He also gave him a big tip, and said, "It was a fine dinner. I really enjoyed it. How about you boys?"

And the waiter said in a voice without strength, "Well, I'm very happy."

When we left, John and I turned to look. The waiter was still at the table. His head was bowed and he was resting with both hands braced on the back of a chair.

Exploring the Ideas

the setting

This story takes place in an expensive New York restaurant. For each of the following indicate if it is typical or unusual for such a restaurant. If you have never actually been in such a restaurant, indicate what you would expect to be typical or unusual.

1. Customers usually wear fancy clothes.
2. The waiters wear suits.
3. Soup and salad is served before the main course.
4. The number of dishes is kept to a minimum so as to reduce costs.
5. Each course is brought on a separate plate.
6. A waiter does his job even if the customer is unhappy.
7. Any conflict between a waiter and customer is resolved as quietly as possible.

Now indicate which of these is common in a restaurant in your country. What customs are typical in restaurants in your country but not in the United States?

the plot

The following list describes things that Robert Laxalt's father did at the exclusive New York restaurant. For each one indicate if it is appropriate or inappropriate behavior in an expensive restaurant.

1. He stared at everyone in the café.
2. He used his thumb and forefinger to ask for a glass of wine.
3. He did not let the waiter take his salad plate.
4. He apologized to the waiter for not letting him take his plate.
5. He cleared the crumbs from the table.
6. He put his passport and wallet bundle on the table.
7. He gave the waiter a large tip.
8. He told the waiter it was a fine dinner.

the theme

Why do you think the father acted the way he did? Do you think he would act the same way if he came to the restaurant a second time? Why do you think so?

How do you think the waiter felt during the incident? Cite specific things from the text that support your idea.

Exploring the Language

vocabulary

Use the following reminders of situations in the story and information to guess the meaning of the words in italics.

1. "And yet, in spite of this *scrutiny*, my father was not *ill at ease*. (line 13)
   What did the people do as the father entered? So *scrutiny* means. . . .
   This did not bother his father, who proceeded to watch the people around him. So *ill at ease* means. . . .

2. "The waiters seemed to *intrigue* him the most." (line 18)
   The father watched the waiters continuously. So *intrigue* means. . . .
3. "It was inevitable that my father's first *altercation* would be with the waiter." (line 22)
   What does the father do when the waiter comes to take the salad plates? So *altercation* means. . . .
4. "He [the waiter] looked at us in something akin to *frenzy*." (line 45)
   Akin means close to. The waiter had probably never had a similar experience and wasn't sure what to do. So *frenzy* means. . . .
5. "And later, when he brought us the check, he stood by with *inscrutable* countenance as my father pulled his passport and wallet bundle out of his pocket, set it on the table, unwound the black inner-tube band, untied the string, and gave him the money." (line 81)
   Countenance is an expression on a face. What do you think the facial expression of the waiter would be like at this time?

descriptive language

Laxalt describes several things by comparing them with something else. For each of the following phrases, indicate how the things being compared are similar.

1. The father's "hands looked more like darkened wood than flesh."
2. The father sat in the restaurant "as if he were in a darkened movie house."
3. The father's expression "was as rapt as a child's."

spoken english

List the phrases that the waiter says to the father when he tries to take his salad plate. Which words make his statements polite and formal?

The father agrees at the end to give the waiter his plate. He says to his son:

> "Well, hell. Tell him to take it then."

Then he says to the waiter:

> "I'm sorry, poor fellow. I didn't know you was that close to losing your job."

Which phrases make these very informal?

idioms

The passage includes several idioms. For example, the father uses his thumb and forefinger to order "a short one." How much wine do you think he wants?

Later, when John is talking to his father, he takes "a deep drag on his cigarette." What do you think "drag" means in this context?

Finally, John warns his father that the waiter could get "fired on the spot." How soon do you think he could get fired?

photo: Floyd K. Takeuchi.

"AT THE WESTERN PALACE"

Maxine Hong Kingston

In this chapter from her autobiography, The Woman Warrior, *Maxine Hong Kingston refers to her mother by name, Brave Orchid. The author herself is one of the American children Brave Orchid has brought with her to the airport.*

When she was about sixty-eight years old Brave Orchid took a day off to wait at San Francisco International Airport for the plane that was bringing her sister to the United States. She had not seen Moon Orchid for thirty years. She had begun this waiting at home, getting up a half-hour before Moon Orchid's plane took off in Hong Kong. Brave Orchid would add her will power to the forces that keep an airplane up. Her head hurt with the concentration. The plane had to be light, so no matter how tired she felt, she dared not rest her spirit on a wing but continuously and gently pushed up on the plane's belly. She had already been waiting at the airport for nine hours. She was wakeful.

Next to Brave Orchid sat Moon Orchid's only daughter, who was helping her aunt wait. Brave Orchid had made two of her own children come too because they could drive, but they had been lured away by the magazine racks and the gift shops and coffee shops. Her American children could not sit for very long. They did not understand sitting; they had wandering feet. She hoped they would get back from the pay t.v.'s or the pay toilets or wherever they were spending their money before the plane arrived. If they did not come back soon, she would go look for them. If her son thought he could hide in the men's room, he was wrong.

"Are you all right, Aunt?" asked her niece.

"No, this chair hurts me. Help me pull some chairs together so I can put my feet up."

She unbundled a blanket and spread it out to make a bed for herself. On the floor she had two shopping bags full of canned peaches, real peaches, beans wrapped in taro leaves, cookies, Thermos bottles, enough food for everybody, though only her niece would eat with her. Her bad boy and bad girl were probably sneaking hamburgers, wasting their money. She would scold them.

Many soldiers and sailors sat about, oddly calm, like little boys in cowboy uniforms. (She thought "cowboy" was what you would call a Boy Scout.) They should have been crying hysterically on their way to Vietnam. "If I see one that looks Chinese," she thought, "I'll go over and give him some advice." She sat up suddenly; she had forgotten about her own son, who was even now in Vietnam. Carefully she split her attention, beaming half of it to the ocean, into the water to keep him afloat. He was on a ship. He was in Vietnamese waters. She was sure of it. He and the other children were lying to her. They had said he was in Japan, and then they said he was in the Philippines. But when she sent him her help, she could feel that he was on a ship in Da Nang. Also she had seen the children hide the envelopes that his letters came in.

"Do you think my son is in Vietnam?" she asked her niece, who was dutifully eating.

"No. Didn't your children say he was in the Philippines?"

"Have you ever seen any of his letters with Philippine stamps on them?"

"Oh, yes. Your children showed me one."

"I wouldn't put it past them to send the letters to some Filipino they know. He puts Manila postmarks on them to fool me."

"Yes, I can imagine them doing that. But don't worry. Your son can take care of himself. All your children can take care of themselves."

"Not him. He's not like other people. Not normal at all. He sticks erasers in his ears, and the erasers are still attached to the pencil stubs. The captain will say, 'Abandon ship,' or, 'Watch out for bombs,' and he won't hear. He doesn't listen to orders. I told him to flee to Canada, but he wouldn't go."

She closed her eyes. After a short while, plane and ship under control, she looked again at the children in uniforms. Some of the blond ones looked like baby chicks, their crew cuts like the downy yellow on baby chicks. You had to feel sorry for them even though they were Army and Navy Ghosts.

Suddenly her son and daughter came running. "Come, Mother. The plane's landed early. She's here already." They hurried, folding up their mother's encampment. She was glad her children were not useless. They must have known what this trip to San Francisco was about then. "It's a good thing I made you come early," she said.

Brave Orchid pushed to the front of the crowd. She had to be in front. The passengers were separated from the people waiting for them by glass doors and walls. Immigration Ghosts were stamping papers. The travellers crowded along some conveyor belts to have their luggage searched. Brave Orchid did not see her sister anywhere. She stood watching for four hours. Her children left and came back. "Why don't you sit down?" they asked.

"The chairs are too far away," she said.

"Why don't you sit on the floor then?"

No, she would stand, as her sister was probably standing in a line she could not see from here. Her American children had no feelings and no memory.

To while away time, she and her niece talked about the Chinese passengers. These new immigrants had it easy. On Ellis Island the people were thin after forty days at sea and had no fancy luggage.

"That one looks like her," Brave Orchid would say.

"No, that's not her."

Ellis Island had been made out of wood and iron. Here everything was new plastic, a ghost trick to lure immigrants into feeling safe and spilling their secrets. Then the Alien Office could send them right back. Otherwise, why did they lock her out, not letting her help her sister answer questions and spell her name? At Ellis Island when the ghost asked Brave Orchid what year her husband had cut off his pigtail, a Chinese who was crouching on the floor motioned her not to talk. "I don't know," she had said. If it weren't for that Chinese man, she might not be here today, or her husband either. She hoped some Chinese, a janitor or a clerk, would look out for Moon Orchid. Luggage conveyors fooled immigrants into thinking the Gold Mountain was going to be easy.

Brave Orchid felt her heart jump—Moon Orchid. "There she is," she shouted. But her niece saw it was not her mother at all. And it shocked her to discover the woman her aunt was pointing out. This was a young woman, younger than herself, no older than Moon Orchid the day the sisters parted. "Moon Orchid will have changed a little, of course," Brave Orchid was saying. "She will have learned to wear western clothes." The woman wore a navy blue suit with a bunch of dark cherries at the shoulder.

"No, Aunt," said the niece. "That's not my mother."

"Perhaps not. It's been so many years. Yes, it is your mother. It must be. Let her come closer, and we can tell. Do you think she's too far away for me to tell, or is it my eyes getting bad?"

"It's too many years gone by," said the niece.

Brave Orchid turned suddenly—another Moon Orchid, this one a neat little woman with a bun. She was laughing at something the person ahead of her in line said. Moon Orchid was just like that, laughing at nothing. "I would be able to tell the difference if one of them would only come closer," Brave Orchid said with tears, which she did not wipe. Two children met the woman with the cherries, and she shook their hands. The other woman was met by a young man. They looked at each other gladly, then walked away side by side.

Up close neither one of those women looked like Moon Orchid at all. "Don't worry, Aunt," said the niece. "I'll know her."

"I'll know her too. I knew her before you did."
The niece said nothing, although she had seen her mother only five years ago. Her aunt liked having the last word.

Finally Brave Orchid's children quit wandering and drooped on a railing. Who knew what they were thinking? At last the niece called out, "I see her! I see her! Mother! Mother!" Whenever the doors parted, she shouted, probably embarrassing the American cousins, but she didn't care. She called out, "Mama! Mama!" until the crack in the sliding doors became too small to let in her voice. "Mama!" What a strange word in an adult voice. Many people turned to see what adult was calling, "Mama!" like a child. Brave Orchid saw an old, old woman jerk her head up, her little eyes blinking confusedly, a woman whose nerves leapt toward the sound anytime she heard "Mama!" Then she relaxed to her own business again. She was a tiny, tiny lady, very thin, with little fluttering hands, and her hair was in a gray knot. She was dressed in a gray wool suit; she wore pearls around her neck and in her earlobes. Moon Orchid *would* travel with her jewels showing. Brave Orchid momentarily saw, like a larger, younger outline around this old woman, the sister she had been waiting for. The familiar dim halo faded, leaving the woman so old, so gray. So old. Brave Orchid pressed against the glass. *That* old lady? Yes, that old lady facing the ghost who stamped her papers without questioning her was her sister. Then, without noticing her family, Moon Orchid walked smiling over to the Suitcase Inspector Ghost, who took her boxes apart, pulling out puffs of tissue. From where she was, Brave Orchid could not see what her sister had chosen to carry across the ocean. She wished her sister would look her way. Brave Orchid thought that if *she* were entering a new country, she would be at the windows. Instead Moon Orchid hovered over the unwrapping, surprised at each reappearance as if she were opening presents after a birthday party.

"Mama!" Moon Orchid's daughter kept calling. Brave Orchid said to her children, "Why don't you call your aunt too? Maybe she'll hear us if all of you call out together." But her children slunk away. Maybe that shame-face they so often wore was American politeness.

"Mama!" Moon Orchid's daughter called again, and this time her mother looked right at her. She left her bundles in a heap and came running. "Hey!" the Customs Ghost yelled at her. She went back to clear up her mess, talking inaudibly to her daughter all the while. Her daughter pointed toward Brave Orchid. And at last Moon Orchid looked at her—two old women with faces like mirrors.

Their hands reached out as if to touch the other's face, then returned to their own, the fingers checking the grooves in the forehead and along the side of the mouth. Moon Orchid, who never understood the gravity of things, started smiling and laughing, pointing at Brave Orchid. Finally Moon Orchid gathered up her stuff, strings hanging and papers loose, and met her sister at the door, where they shook hands, oblivious to blocking the way.

"You're an old woman," said Brave Orchid.

"Aiaa. *You're* an old woman."

"But you are really old. Surely, you can't say that about me. I'm not old the way you're old."

"But *you* really are old. You're one year older than I am."

"Your hair is white and your face all wrinkled."

"You're so skinny."

"You're so fat."

"Fat women are more beautiful than skinny women."

The children pulled them out of the doorway. One of Brave Orchid's children brought the car from the parking lot, and the other heaved the luggage into the trunk. They put the two old ladies and the niece in the back seat. All the way home—across the Bay Bridge, over the Diablo hills, across the San Joaquin River to the valley, the valley moon so white at dusk—all the way home, the two sisters exclaimed every time they turned to look at each other, "Aiaa! How old!"

Brave Orchid forgot that she got sick in cars, that all vehicles but palanquins made her dizzy. "You're so old," she kept saying. "How did you get so old?"

Brave Orchid had tears in her eyes. But Moon Orchid said, "You look older than I. You *are* older than I," and again she'd laugh. "You're wearing an old mask to tease me." It surprised Brave Orchid that after thirty years she could still get annoyed at her sister's silliness.

Exploring the Ideas

characterization

Sometimes the story tells why Brave Orchid acted as she did at the airport in words that sound as though Brave Orchid herself were speaking. Which of the following actions does the story explain fully? What were the reasons? For unexplained or partially explained actions, can you suggest a reason from what the rest of the story has told you about her?

1. Brave Orchid got up a half-hour before Moon Orchid's plane took off in Hong Kong.

2. She made her two children come to the airport.
3. She brought food to the airport.
4. She pushed to the front of the crowd when the plane arrived.
5. She stood and waited for four hours for her sister to pass through customs.

The author at times also tells us directly how Brave Orchid feels. For example, in the first paragraph, the author writes of Brave Orchid, "Her head hurt with the concentration." Find other examples of times when the author comments on Brave Orchid's feelings.

the theme

The 68-year-old Brave Orchid has many indirect criticisms of American life. Indicate what she is criticizing in each of the following lines.

1. "Many soldiers and sailors sat about, oddly calm, like little boys in cowboy uniforms. . . . They should have been crying hysterically on their way to Vietnam."
2. "Some of the blond ones [soldiers] looked like baby chicks, their crew cuts like the downy yellow on baby chicks."
3. "Ellis Island had been made out of wood and iron. Here [at the airport] everything was new plastic, a ghost trick to lure immigrants into feeling safe and spilling their secrets." (Ellis Island is an island in upper New York Bay that used to be the chief United States immigration station.)
4. "Luggage conveyors fooled immigrants into thinking Gold Mountain was going to be easy." (Many immigrants came to California in the mid-19th century in search of gold. What do you think Gold Mountain refers to?)
5. "Brave Orchid forgot that she got sick in cars, that all vehicles but palanquins made her dizzy." (A palanquin is a covered chair that is carried on poles on the shoulders of two or four men.)

The subtitle of *Woman Warrior* is *Memoirs of a Girlhood Among Ghosts.* Why do you think military personnel and immigration officials are called ghosts?

During the 1911 Xing Hai Revolution in China many men cut off their pigtails in protest against the Ching dynasty. Why do you think the immigration official at Ellis Island asked Brave Orchid when her husband had cut off his pigtail? If he had done it in 1911, what might the official have assumed? Why do you think the Chinese who was sitting on the floor motioned for her not to talk?

It takes Moon Orchid four hours to go through customs but her papers are stamped without any questions. If you went through immigration, at what entry point did you go through? How long did it take? What questions were you asked?

Exploring the Language

word associations

In English some words have positive connotations or associations such as the word "persistent," while other words have negative connotations such as the words "stubborn" or "obstinate." The following sentences all describe Brave Orchid's thoughts about her children. Which words do not have good connotations?

1. "They had been lured away by the magazine racks." (line 14)
2. "They did not understand sitting; they had wandering feet." (line 16)
3. "Her bad boy and bad girl were probably sneaking hamburgers, wasting their money." (line 29)
4. "I wouldn't put it past them to send the letter to some Filipino they know. He puts Manila postmarks on them to fool me." (line 50)
5. "He's not like other people. Not normal at all." (line 55)
6. "Brave Orchid said to her children, 'Why don't you call your aunt too? Maybe she'll hear us if all of you call out together.' But her children slunk away. Maybe that shame-face they so often wore was American politeness." (line 154)

vocabulary

Use the following reminders of situations in the story and the information on word parts to guess the meaning of the following words.

1. "They hurried, folding up their mother's *encampment.*" (line 66) What does Brave Orchid bring to the airport with her? They are putting these things away. So an *encampment* is . . .
2. Moon Orchid "went back to clear up her mess, talking *inaudibly* to her daughter all the while." (line 159)
   In means not and *audible* means able to be heard. What do you think inaudibly means? How can Moon Orchid talk to her daughter inaudibly?

3. "Instead Moon Orchid *hovered* over the unwrappings, surprised at each reappearance as if she were opening presents after a birthday party." (line 150)
   Brave Orchid wished that her sister would look her way, but she doesn't. Instead, she looks over the things she brought as if they were presents. So *hovering* means. . .

stressed words

Why do you think the author italicized certain words in the following sentences? How would you say these sentences?

1. "Moon Orchid *would* travel with her jewels showing." (line 138)
2. "*That* old lady? Yes, that old lady facing the ghost who stamped her papers without questioning her was her sister." (line 142)
3. "She wished her sister would look her way. Brave Orchid thought that if *she* were entering a new country, she would be at the windows." (line 149)
4. "'You're an old woman,' said Brave Orchid.
   'Aiaa. *You're* an old woman.'
   'But *you* are really old. Surely, you can't say that about me. I'm not old the way you're old.'
   'But *you* really are old. You're one year older than I am.'" (line 170)
5. "But Moon Orchid said, 'You look older than I. You *are* older than I.'" (line 190)

sentence modifiers

Several sentences in the passage include a special type of noun modifier composed of a noun and a participle. For each of the following sentences, rewrite the italicized phrase so it is a complete sentence. Notice how writing the information as a separate sentence makes the idea less integrated.

1. "After a short while, *plane and ship under control*, she looked again at the children in uniforms." (line 60)
2. "Brave Orchid saw an old, old woman jerk her head up, *her little eyes blinking confusedly*." (line 132)
3. "Their hands reached out as if to touch the other's face, then returned to their own, *the fingers checking the grooves in the forehead and along the side of the mouth*." (line 163)
4. "Finally Moon Orchid gathered up her stuff, *strings hanging and papers loose*, and met her sister at the door." (line 167)

photo: California Historical Library Society.

"THE HUNDRED-YEAR-OLD MAN"

Maxine Hong Kingston

China Men, the story from which this selection is taken, describes the lives of Chinese immigrant men in the United States. In this word portrait, Maxine Hong Kingston honors a man who knows what joy is.

THERE IS A MAN WHO WOULD BE ONE HUNDRED AND SEVENTEEN YEARS OLD NOW. He had a one-hundred-and-sixth birthday party in the Palolo Chinese Home in Hawai'i in 1969. He wore a wool cap. He told the guests he came to Hawai'i in 1885 on the S.S. *Coptic.* He brought with him pigs in cages, and chives and onions growing in cans. He had divided his ration of fresh water with the pigs, the chives, and the onions.

He worked in the sugarcane fields for four dollars a month, and his first job had been to clear the brush for planting. He lived in a grass house, but later moved into a dormitory, where he slept in a bunk covered with grass mats. He sent one half of his pay to his family in China. Here's how he spent the rest: He bought kerosene and wood; he paid off some of his debts, his passage to Hawai'i, and the twelve-dollar fee for processing his papers; he spent six dollars to join his Benevolent Association, which gave him room and board when he took his monthly trip to Honolulu on pay day. He rode to town in a horse cart for thirty cents; it carried five passengers. When he could not afford the thirty cents, he walked.

He rested by smoking opium, which the plantation foreman sold. A half-hour's worth of high was called a dragon seed and cost fifty cents. When Hawai'i outlawed opium, he switched to cigars.

He saw King Kalakaua and Prince Kuhio. In 1893 he did not go to town because of the American revolution against Queen Lili'uokalani, who was "big and friendly," he said. "I was for the Americans," he added.

Since 1885 he has left the island twice, once to go to Maui and once to Kaua'i.

On this one-hundred-and-sixth birthday, the United States was still fighting in Vietnam, and people asked him how to stop the war. "Let everybody out of the army," he said.

"In one hundred and six years, what has given you the most joy?" the reporters asked.

He thought it over. He said, "What I like best is to work in a cane field when the young green plants are just growing up."

"In the end," said Tu Fu, "I will carry a hoe."

Exploring the Ideas

The passage opens with the sentence: "There is a man who would be one hundred and seventeen years old now." What does this indicate about the man? When was the passage written?

How old was the hundred-year-old man when he came to Hawaii? How many years had he spent in Hawaii by the time of his one-hundred-and-sixth birthday? Where did he spend his one-hundred-and-sixth birthday? Who do you think the guests were? Why do you think a reporter was present?

The passage describes the hundred-year-old man's life in Hawaii. The following list describes things he did. For each one, give an adjective that might be used to characterize his behavior. In many cases more than one adjective may be appropriate.

Example

Action: He sent one half of his pay to his family in China.
Characteristic: generous, concerned

1. When he could not afford to ride to town, he walked.
2. He rested by smoking opium.
3. When opium was outlawed, he switched to cigars.
4. Since 1885 he had left the island twice to visit two other Hawaiian islands.
5. His solution to the Vietnam war was to let everyone out of the army.
6. His greatest joy was to work in a cane field.

Suppose the hundred-year-old man went to the exclusive New York restaurant where the father of Robert Laxalt went. How do you think he would have acted? Why do you think so?

Suppose the hundred-year-old man were to greet his brother at the San Francisco airport like Brave Orchid. How do you think he would have acted? Why do you think so?

In the last paragraph, the author comments on the hundred-year-old man's life by quoting a famous Chinese poet, Tu Fu. Why do you think she chose that quotation?

Composing

defining by example: making and supporting a generalization

The three passages from *Sweet Promised Land, The Woman Warrior,* and *China Men* all describe older people who have lived in the United States for a considerable length of time. Write an essay in which you discuss whether or not they are typical Americans. Begin the essay by listing three or four characteristics that you believe are shared by most Americans (i.e., citizens of the United States). For example, you may believe that most Americans are status conscious or casual or outspoken. Include your reasons for listing the characteristics that you do.

In the next section of the essay, indicate if you think Robert Laxalt's father, Brave Orchid, and/or the hundred-year-old man demonstrate these characteristics. Be sure to use specific examples from the stories which show the characters do or do not have the attributes that you believe are shared by most Americans.

photo: The Metropolitan Museum of Art, Rogers Fund, 1925.

"SHIKATA GA NAI"

Jeanne Wakatsuki Houston
James D. Houston

This chapter is taken from an autobiography entitled Farewell to Manzanar *by Jeanne Wakatsuki Houston and her husband, James Houston. In 1942 when the author was seven years old, she and her family were sent to live at Manzanar internment camp, located in Owens Valley, California. After the bombing of Pearl Harbor, Japanese immigrants on the West Coast were sent to live in special internment camps, based on groundless fears that they might threaten the war effort. In this chapter Mrs. Houston's father has already been arrested and taken away. (Woody is her older brother and Chizu is his wife.)*

In December of 1941 Papa's disappearance didn't bother me nearly so much as the world I soon found myself in.

He had been a jack-of-all trades. When I was born he was farming near Inglewood. Later, when he started fishing, we moved to Ocean Park, near Santa Monica, and until they picked him up, that's where we lived, in a big frame house with a brick fireplace, a block back from the beach. We were the only Japanese family in the neighborhood. Papa liked it that way. He didn't want to be labeled or grouped by anyone. But with him gone and no way of knowing what to expect, my mother moved all of us down to Terminal Island. Woody already lived there, and one of my older sisters had married a Terminal Island boy. Mama's first concern now was to keep the family together; and once the war began, she felt safer there than isolated racially in Ocean Park. But for me, at age seven, the island was a country as foreign as India or Arabia would have been. It was the first time I had lived among other Japanese, or gone to school with them, and I was terrified all the time.

This was partly Papa's fault. One of his threats to keep us younger kids in line was "I'm going to sell you to the Chinaman." When I had entered kindergarten two years earlier, I was the only Oriental in the class. They sat me next to a Caucasian girl who happened to have very slanted eyes. I looked at her and began to scream, certain Papa had sold me out at last. My fear of her ran so deep I could not speak of it, even to Mama, couldn't explain why I was screaming. For two weeks I had nightmares about this girl, until the teachers finally moved me to the other side of the room. And it was still with me, this fear of Oriental faces, when we moved to Terminal Island.

In those days it was a company town, a ghetto owned and controlled by the canneries. The men went after fish, and whenever the boats came back—day or night—the women would be called to process the catch while it was fresh. One in the afternoon or four in the morning, it made no difference. My mother had to go to work right after we moved there. I can still hear the whistle—two toots for French's, three for Van Camp's—and she and Chizu would be out of bed in the middle of the night, heading for the cannery.

The house we lived in was nothing more than a shack, a barracks with single plank walls and rough wooden floors, like the cheapest kind of migrant workers' housing. The people around us were hard-working, boisterous, a little proud of their nickname, *yo-go-re*, which meant literally *uncouth one*, or roughneck, or dead-end kid. They not only spoke Japanese exclusively, they spoke a dialect peculiar to Kyushu, where their families had come from in Japan, a rough, fisherman's language, full of oaths and insults. Instead of saying *ba-ka-ta-re*, a common insult meaning *stupid*, Terminal Islanders would say *ba-ka-ya-ro*, a coarser and exclusively masculine use of the word, which implies gross stupidity. They would swagger and pick on outsiders and persecute anyone who didn't speak as they did. That was what made my own time there so hateful. I had never spoken anything but English, and the other kids in the second grade despised me for it. They were tough and mean, like ghetto kids anywhere. Each day after school I dreaded their ambush. My brother Kiyo, three years older, would wait for me at the door, where we would decide whether to run straight home together, or split up, or try a new and unexpected route.

None of these kids ever actually attacked. It was the threat that frightened us, their fearful looks, and the noises they would make, like miniature Samurai, in a language we couldn't understand.

At the time it seemed we had been living under this reign of fear for years. In fact, we lived there about two months. Late in February the navy decided to clear Terminal Island completely. Even though most of us were American-born, it was dangerous having that many Orientals so close to the Long Beach Naval Station, on the opposite end of the island. We had known something like this was coming. But, like Papa's arrest, not much could be done ahead of time. There were four of us kids still young enough to be living with Mama, plus Granny, her mother, sixty-five then, speaking no English, and nearly blind. Mama didn't know where else she could get work, and we had nowhere else to move *to*. On February 25 the choice was made for us. We were given forty-eight hours to clear out.

The secondhand dealers had been prowling around for weeks, like wolves, offering humiliating prices for goods and furniture they knew many of us would have to sell sooner or later. Mama had left all but her most valuable possessions in Ocean Park, simply because she had nowhere to put them. She had brought along her pottery, her silver, heirlooms like the kimonos Granny had brought from Japan, tea sets, lacquered tables, and one fine old set of china, blue and white porcelain, almost translucent. On the day we were leaving, Woody's car was so crammed with boxes and luggage and kids we had just run out of room. Mama had to sell this china.

One of the dealers offered her fifteen dollars for it. She said it was a full setting for twelve and worth at least two hundred. He said fifteen was his top price. Mama started to quiver. Her eyes blazed up at him. She had been packing all night and trying to calm down Granny, who didn't understand why we were moving again and what all the rush was about. Mama's nerves were shot, and now navy jeeps were patrolling the streets. She didn't say another word. She just glared at this man, all the rage and frustration channeled at him through her eyes.

He watched her for a moment and said he was sure he couldn't pay more than seventeen fifty for that china. She reached into the red velvet case, took out a dinner plate and hurled it at the floor right in front of his feet.

The man leaped back shouting, "Hey! Hey, don't do that! Those are valuable dishes!"

Mama took out another dinner plate and hurled it at the floor, then another and another, never moving, never opening her mouth, just quivering and glaring at the retreating dealer, with tears streaming down her cheeks. He finally turned and scuttled out the door, heading for the next house. When he was gone she stood there smashing cups and bowls and platters until the whole set lay in scattered blue and white fragments across the wooden floor.

Exploring the Ideas

the setting

The chapter describes various aspects of Terminal Island. Which of the following statements accurately describe the island? Which are inaccurate descriptions? Correct those that are inaccurate.

1. The town was controlled by canneries.
2. The women would process the fish at regular hours.
3. There were two canneries in the town, French's and Van Camp's.
4. The family lived in run-down housing.
5. The people of the island spoke a standard Japanese dialect.

6. The people of the island would pick on anyone who did not speak their dialect.
7. The other children of the island often attacked the author.
8. Terminal Island was close to Long Beach Naval Station.

the theme

ACCULTURATION. The author's father was born and spent his first seventeen years in Japan, yet he liked the fact that they were the only Japanese family in Ocean Park, California. Why do you think he preferred living with non-Japanese? Why do you think he told his children, "I'm going to sell you to the Chinaman"? Considering the problems that the author had at Terminal Island, do you think he should have taught his children Japanese?

The fact that the author grew up in an environment without other Japanese families created several problems for her. When she entered kindergarten, how did she react to a Caucasian girl who had Oriental features? How did she feel at Terminal Island? How did the other students at the Terminal Island school treat her? Why do you think they did this?

EXPLOITATION. The author's mother brought only her most valuable possessions to Terminal Island. Among them was a set of china, including bowls like the one in the picture. Since she had no room to take it with her, she tried to sell it. What did she believe the set was worth? When the dealer would give her no more than $17.50, why do you think she threw one of the plates on the floor? Why do you think she continued to throw them even after he left? The chapter title, "Shikata Ga Nai," means "it can't be helped." Why do you think the author gave it this title?

Exploring the Language

descriptive verbs

The passage uses very specific verbs to describe the action of the characters. Use the context clues in the sentences, and what you know about the characters and the story to match the italicized verbs with the definitions listed below.

1. Terminal Islanders "would *swagger* and pick on outsiders and persecute anyone who didn't speak as they did." (line 47)

2. "The secondhand dealers had been *prowling* around for weeks, like wolves, offering humiliating prices for goods and furniture they knew many of us would have to sell sooner or later." (line 71)
3. Mama "just *glared* at this man, all the rage and frustration channeled at him through her eyes." (line 87)
4. Mama "reached into the red velvet case, took out a dinner plate and *hurled* it at the floor right in front of his feet." (line 91)
5. "The man *leaped* back shouting, 'Hey! Hey!, don't do that!'" line 94)
6. "He finally turned and *scuttled* out the door, heading for the next house." (line 99)

Definitions

a. to stare angrily
b. to walk in a boastful manner
c. to throw with great force
d. to run hastily
e. to roam as in search of prey
f. to move quickly

vocabulary

Use the following information and reminders of situations in the story to guess the meaning of the terms in italics.

1. "Each day after school I dreaded their *ambush*." (line 52)
   The other second-grade students despised her for not speaking their language. What do you think she believes will happen on her way home from school? So *ambush* means. . . .
2. "It was the threat that frightened us, their fearful looks, and the noises they would make, like miniature *Samurai*, in a language we couldn't understand." (line 56)
   Samurai are a group of men of ancient Japan. The author compares the other second-grade students' threats, looks and noises to Samurai. What kind of people do you think the Samurai were?
3. Mama "had brought along her pottery, her silver, *heirlooms* like the kimonos Granny had brought from Japan. . . ." (line 75)
   The author's mother brought only her most valuable possessions with her. One example of a *heirloom* is her mother's kimonos that had belonged to her grandmother. So *heirloom* means. . . .

photo: California Historical Society by Maisir & Richard Conrat.

from I KNOW WHY THE CAGED BIRD SINGS

Maya Angelou

Maya Angelou came from Stamps, Arkansas, as a teen-ager to live in San Francisco's Fillmore District. The district was undergoing a rapid change because of the internment of Japanese-Americans. These included the Nisei, or second-generation Japanese like Jeanne Wakatsuki Houston, born and educated in the United States.

IN THE EARLY MONTHS OF WORLD WAR II, San Francisco's Fillmore district, or the Western Addition, experienced a visible revolution. On the surface it appeared to be totally peaceful and almost a refutation of the term "revolution."

The Yakamoto Sea Food Market quietly became Sammy's Shoe Shine Parlor and Smoke Shop. Yashigira's Hardware metamorphosed into La Salon de Beauté owned by Miss Clorinda Jackson. The Japanese shops which sold products to Nisei customers were taken over by enterprising Negro businessmen, and in less than a year became permanent homes away from home for the newly arrived Southern Blacks. Where the odors of tempura, raw fish and *cha* had dominated, the aroma of chitlings, greens and ham hocks now prevailed.

The Asian population dwindled before my eyes. I was unable to tell the Japanese from the Chinese and as yet found no real difference in the national origin of such sounds as Ching and Chan or Moto and Kano.

As the Japanese disappeared, soundlessly and without protest, the Negroes entered with their loud jukeboxes, their just-released animosities and the relief of escape from Southern bonds. The Japanese area became San Francisco's Harlem in a matter of months.

A person unaware of all the factors that make up oppression might have expected sympathy or even support from the Negro newcomers for the dislodged Japanese. Especially in view of the fact that they (the Blacks) had themselves undergone concentration-camp living for centuries in slavery's plantations and later in sharecroppers' cabins. But the sensations of common relationship were missing.

The Black newcomer had been recruited on the dessicated farm lands of Georgia and Mississippi by war-plant labor scouts. The chance to live in two- or three-story apartment buildings (which became instant slums), and to earn two- and even three-figured weekly checks, was blinding. For the first time he could think of himself as a

Boss, a Spender. He was able to pay other people to work for him, i.e. the dry cleaners, taxi drivers, waitresses, etc. The shipyards and ammunition plants brought to booming life by the war let him know that he was needed and even appreciated. A completely alien yet very pleasant position for him to experience. Who could expect this man to share his new and dizzying importance with concern for a race that he had never known to exist?

Another reason for his indifference to the Japanese removal was more subtle but was more profoundly felt. The Japanese were not whitefolks. Their eyes, language and customs belied the white skin and proved to their dark successors that since they didn't have to be feared, neither did they have to be considered. All this was decided unconsciously.

No member of my family and none of the family friends ever mentioned the absent Japanese. It was as if they had never owned or lived in the houses we inhabited. On Post Street, where our house was, the hill skidded slowly down to Fillmore, the market heart of our district. In the two short blocks before it reached its destination, the street housed two day-and-night restaurants, two pool halls, four Chinese restaurants, two gambling houses, plus diners, shoeshine shops, beauty salons, barber shops and at least four churches. To fully grasp the never-ending activity in San Francisco's Negro neighborhood during the war, one need only know that the two blocks described were side streets that were duplicated many times over in the eight- to ten-square-block area.

Exploring the Ideas

the theme

The passage from *I Know Why the Caged Bird Sings* describes several changes in the Western Addition of San Francisco that were brought about by World War II. Because of the creation of internment camps, many Japanese were forced to leave the area. Their homes and shops were then bought by Blacks who came from the South to find jobs in the war factories. Whereas in 1940 fewer than 5,000 Blacks lived in San Francisco, by 1950 their numbers had grown to 43,000. In order to explore these changes, refer to the chapter to identify what replaced each of the following.

Example

Quiet Japanese were replaced by
Blacks with loud jukeboxes.

1. The Yakamoto Sea Food Market
2. Yashigira's Hardware
3. Japanese shops
4. Odors of tempura, raw fish and cha

The author, Maya Angelou, points out that since the Blacks had suffered the humiliation of slavery, one might assume that they would be sympathetic to the plight of the Japanese. Yet this was not the case. What are two reasons she mentions as to why the Blacks generally did not show sympathy for the homeless Japanese?

Exploring the Language

verbs

On several occasions Maya Angelou uses verbs in ways they are typically not used. Notice the following examples.

1. "The chance to live in two- or three-story apartment buildings. . . and to earn two- or even three-figured weekly checks, was *blinding*." (line 29)
   In which of the following ways is the term *blind* used?
   a. to deprive of sight
   b. to overwhelm
   c. to darken
   d. to deprive a person of his judgement
2. "On Post Street, where our house was, the hill *skidded* slowly down to Fillmore, the market heart of our district." (line 48)
   To skid means to slide or slip. What things usually *skid*? Why do you think the author states that the hill skidded?

Use the following reminders of the context and information to guess the meaning of the verbs in italics.

3. "Yashigira's Hardware Store *metamorphosed* into La Salon de Beauté owned by Miss Clorinda Jackson." (line 6)
   What do you think happened to Yashigira's Hardware Store? So *metamorphose* means to. . . .
4. "The Asian population *dwindled* before my eyes." (line 14)
   At the beginning of World War II many Japanese were moved to internment camps. So *dwindle* means. . . .
5. "Their eyes, language and customs *belied* the white skin and proved to their dark successors that since they didn't have to be feared, neither did they have to be considered." (line 42)

To lie, of course, means to present false information. *Be* is a prefix that indicates the existence of a condition. So *belie* means. . . .

adjectives

Two common endings of adjectives are *ed* and *ing*. Use the following information and reminders of the context to guess the meaning of the adjectives in italics.

1. "The Japanese shops which sold products to Nisei customers were taken over by *enterprising* Negro businessmen, and in less than a year became permanent homes away from home for the newly arrived Southern Blacks." (line 8)
   In less than a year the Negro businessmen were able to get enough business so that they could stay permanently in the Western Addition. So *enterprising* means. . . .
2. "A person unaware of all the factors that make up oppression might have expected sympathy or even support from the Negro newcomers for the *dislodged* Japanese." (line 22)
   To lodge, of course, means to stay in a place. One meaning of the prefix *dis* is a lack of. So *dislodged* means. . . .
3. "The Black newcomer had been recruited on the *dessicated* farm lands of Georgia and Mississippi by war-plant labor scouts." (line 28)
   Many Blacks left their farms to work in the northern war factories because their farms were not yielding good crops. What might cause land not to produce crops? So *dessicate* means. . . .

Composing

describing a place

Maya Angelou describes the changes that occurred in San Francisco during the second world war. As a Black, she probably would not have felt comfortable in the original Western Addition community. She did, however, feel very much a part of the new Western Addition. As she lived in and explored the city of San Francisco, it became quite important to her.

Write an essay in which you describe a place you know well that has undergone tremendous changes. It can be a house, a park, or a section of a city. Describe what it was like in the past and what it is like today. Then indicate which one you prefer—the old or the new—and why.

classifying effects

The internment camps during World War II had widespread effects on both Japanese-Americans and other ethnic groups. Begin by listing some of the changes that are described in the passage from *Farewell to Manzanar* and *I Know Why the Caged Bird Sings*.

For example, what effect did the internment camps have on Jeanne Wakatsuki Houston's mother? On Jeanne herself? On where the family lived and what they did? On what language they spoke?

What effect did the internment camps have on Maya Angelou? On where her family lived and what they did? On the Fillmore district in San Francisco?

Classify these changes into two or three major categories. Then write an essay in which you describe some of the effects of the internment camps. Be sure to use specific details from the texts to illustrate these effects.

photo: National Archives, Washington, D.C.

from TOUCH THE EARTH

From Touch the Earth compiled by T. C. McLuhan (New York: Promontory Press, 1971).

On June 17, 1744, the commissioners from Maryland and Virginia negotiated a treaty with the Indians of the Six Nations at Lancaster, Pennsylvania. The Indians were invited to send boys to William and Mary College. The next day they declined the offer as follows.

WE KNOW THAT YOU HIGHLY ESTEEM THE KIND OF LEARNING taught in those Colleges, and that the Maintenance of our young Men, while with you, would be very expensive to you. We are convinced, that you mean to do us Good by your Proposal; and we thank you heartily. But you, who are wise must know that different Nations have different Conceptions of things and you will therefore not take it amiss, if our Ideas of this kind of Education happen not to be the same as yours. We have had some Experience of it. Several of our young People were formerly brought up at the Colleges of the Northern Provinces: they were instructed in all your Sciences; but, when they came back to us, they were bad Runners, ignorant of every means of living in the woods . . . neither fit for Hunters, Warriors, nor Counsellors, they were totally good for nothing.

We are, however, not the less oblig'd by your kind Offer, tho' we decline accepting it; and, to show our grateful Sense of it, if the Gentlemen of Virginia will send us a Dozen of their Sons, we will take Care of their Education, instruct them in all we know, and make Men of them.

photo: Laura Gilpin Collection, Amon Carter Museum.

from MEDICINE MAN'S DAUGHTER

Ann Nolan Clark

In spite of the Indian chief's eloquence in declining a white man's education for the young men of his tribe, it later became a necessity for Indians to go to schools, established especially for their education. Tall-Girl, the daughter of a Navajo medicine man who has been training her to become a medicine woman, has decided to go to a mission school because the doctors there have saved the life of a baby she loves. Tall-Girl wants to learn the white medicine, too.

WHEN THE BUS MADE ITS NEXT STOP, the driver spoke to the Navajo girl. Not getting an answer, he pulled the blanket from her face. He said to her, "This is where you get off. Do you have a suitcase or something?" Tall-Girl made no answer. She flashed a look at him through her thick eyelashes. He had put his eyes on his face. She got off the bus.

They had stopped at an opening in a high stone wall. Over the opening was a wrought-iron arch with the words "St. Mary's" on it. Tall-Girl looked at it, but she did not know what it was. She could not read. Coming toward her was Grey-Eyes, but not the Grey-Eyes she had known in a long calico skirt and velvet blouse. This Grey-Eyes wore a short skirt and a white blouse with short sleeves. Tall-Girl was shocked. A daughter of The People in such clothes! She looked again. Grey-Eyes' long, beautiful hair was gone. It had been cut in a short, square bob.

Tall-Girl turned to climb back into the bus. It was moving away. She knew she could not catch it.

Grey-Eyes was running toward her, saying in Navajo over and over, "Little dear one." It was the name Elder-Sister often used in speaking to Chanter's daughter. Grey-Eyes hugged her. Tall-Girl was surprised. She had never been hugged before. Navajo touch fingertips in a swift gentle touching to show affectionate greeting.

Then Grey-Eyes smiled. All the strange things were forgotten. The world righted itself. This was Grey-Eyes, her companion for as long as she could remember. This was Grey-Eyes whom she had missed so very much. Her eyes grew bright with tears unshed as she looked at Grey-Eyes, gravely, unsmiling but tenderly.

"Is the night corral where it always has been? Do my sheep miss me now that I am not there to take them to the waterhole?" Grey-Eyes laughing face was serious. This was her way of saying, "Little dear one, look at me. Only the appearance is changed. What I am in my heart is still the daughter of The People." Tall-Girl understood. She understood the words that Grey-Eyes spoke and the ones that were unspoken. Understanding flowed between them, deep and true and lasting.

Grey-Eyes pointed, in the typical Navajo way, lip stuck out, chin uplifted, to the nun who was standing by the opening in the wall. "That one is known as Sister Jean Catherine. She is the headman of the Sister-clan at this place," she explained to Tall-Girl, leading her to the nun who waited for them.

When Tall-Girl reached her, Sister Jean Catherine held out her hand, touching Tall-Girl's fingertips in a way that was Navajo-proper. At once Tall-Girl liked her. The small, correct, welcoming gesture had taken down the blanket-covering from Tall-Girl's heart.

In English Sister Jean Catherine said to Grey-Eyes, "Tell your cousin that St. Mary's Mission School welcomes her. We are glad that she is to be with us."

"Ye', Sister," Grey-Eyes answered. To Tall-Girl she said in Navajo, "They would not have taken you if the Trader had not insisted. He used the telephone box to talk to them." Grey-Eyes looked at Sister Jean Catherine and added to Tall-Girl, "The Trader is important here. The ones who have this school listen to what he says."

Tall-Girl understood this. He was important to her family also. She said, "They know, perhaps, that he has many sheep."

"No," Grey-Eyes answered. "They are not impressed with sheep. They do not even like them. The Trader has words. He uses them until they say yes."

Tall-Girl nodded. She understood this also. The Trader liked to talk.

Sister Jean Catherine was in a hurry. She had many things to do. If it had not been for the Trader's insistence, she would have sent another nun down to the gate to meet the new pupil. She listened to Grey-Eyes talking. It took them so long, she thought, to put the simplest English words into Navajo. It should not take so long to tell the new girl she was welcome. Although the nun neither moved nor spoke, Grey-Eyes sensed her impatience. She smiled at the nun, telling her, "This one says to tell you she is glad to be here. She says to tell you she will learn the English quick."

Sister Jean Catherine was pleased. The new girl had a sense of responsibility, she decided. Grey-Eyes also was pleased. She liked to translate for Sister. It did not bother Grey-Eyes if her interpretation was not exactly what Tall-Girl had said. It was, she thought, what she would have said if she had said it.

Tall-Girl was pleased. This person in the long black dress and the strange-looking shawl over her head was a good person. She knew how to make the proper greeting. The new life had begun in a good way. She looked at the sky. Sun-Carrier with the great sun in his arms had just begun the morning walk across the roof of the world. The girl turned to Grey-Eyes, saying, "Someone sings the sunrise song here. That person is known to you, perhaps."

Grey-Eyes answered, but Tall-Girl did not hear her. Thoughts of Chanter had entered her mind. She felt no anger toward him now. She had only the memory of her anger. How beautiful and strong, she thought, he sings the sunrise song. How beautiful and strong he was in all his actions. The memory of his last words to her pierced her heart, but she would not allow the hurt to remain with her. Grey-Eyes knew that her cousin was thinking of Chanter. She knew that Chanter had not approved her coming. He would never approve it. The wonder was that he had allowed it. But she asked no questions. Tall-Girl gave no explanation.

The nun and the two girls walked up the cottonwood-lined driveway. At its end was a tall, square brick building, ugly and old. It had been school and home for fifty years to the Navajo girls whose parents had allowed them to go to school. The nun saw it with affection and pride. It was no small matter to have a building of its kind right in the heart of the Navajo wastelands. "Substantially built," she thought, "with good square corners and a second story, the only one of its kind in a hundred miles."

Tall-Girl looked at the building in dismay. Except for the Trading Post, it was the first Whiteman building she had seen. She did not like it. She did not think she could live within its walls. It was tall and square with a steep, sloping roof, not domed nor round sun-shaped as a dwelling should be. Its walls were full of windows like ghost eyes, vacant and sightless.

Beside the large building was a smaller one. As they walked toward it, the bell in its tower pealed a clear bell tone into the morning freshness. Tall-Girl was delighted. She had never heard a church bell before. She loved its sound. Almost instantaneous with the bell-pealing, a long line of girls marched from the large buildings to the smaller one. They were dressed as Grey-Eyes was, in short pleated skirts and white middy blouses, the uniform of Saint Mary's.

"Tell her," Sister Jean Catherine said, "that we are going to Mass. We go every morning at six o'clock."

"Ye', Sister," Grey-Eyes said. Turning to Tall-Girl, she translated what Sister had said into, "That's their church. Its where they keep their Yei." Tall-Girl was interested. She quickened her steps. They went into the church behind the line of marching girls.

At Grey-Eyes' nudging, Tall-Girl knelt, stood up, sat down as the other girls did. She took short, darting looks at everything around her, but she could not see much and understood nothing. She pointed her lips at the statues, her gesture asking a question. Grey-Eyes nodded. "Their Yei," she whispered, looking to see if a Sister heard her.

Tall-Girl felt confused and faint. The candles on the altar blurred her sight. In this first visit only two things impressed her, the organ music and the singing of the choir that she listened to in delight. The other thing was vague, unreal. It was the figure of a Man hanging on a piece of wood. She caught only a fleeting glance as she passed by it, but it left a cold uneasiness within her.

From the church they marched with the other girls to the dining room, to sit on long benches, before long tables. Tall-Girl had eaten her meals sitting on the ground beside a cook-fire. She had always been served alone and apart from the others who happened to be eating.

This morning at the table all the girls sat so closely together that constantly their arms touched and bumped together. Tall-Girl was embarrassed to be eating so close to others. She felt ill at ease. She had never seen some of the foods that were on the table. She did not like their taste. She watched the other girls. What they did, she did. What they ate, she ate, and her stomach tied itself in knots.

After the agony of breakfast was over, Grey-Eyes took her to another place. This was to Sister Angelica's office. The nun sat at a desk writing on paper. She spoke to Grey-Eyes.

"She says what is your name?" Grey-Eyes interpreted.

Although it was an impolite thing to ask her, Tall-Girl was ready for it. The Trader had warned her. "Despah Tseghi," she said, looking straight ahead. Grey-Eyes was pleased at her cousin's quick thinking.

The nun looked at the paper she was holding. "The one who signed this application," she told Grey-Eyes, "has another name." Grey-Eyes looked at the paper. Her mother had put her mark on it underneath where the Trader had written her name.

The nun asked, "Is this person her mother?"

"No," Grey-Eyes answered, "my mother. Her mother's sister."

"Why didn't her parents sign the application?"

Grey-Eyes answered, "I don't know."

"Are her parents dead?" The nun looked severely at Grey-Eyes. The girl was worried. She did not want to make it necessary for Tall-Girl to say that her mother was dead. She did not want to bring Chanter into the conversation. She said nothing.

The Sister waited until the silence began to bother her. She tried another way of asking the question. "Ask the new girl," she said to Grey-Eyes, "If her parents are living."

"Ye', Sister," Grey-Eyes smiled. "Perhaps you want to go home," she said in Navajo.

Tall-Girl did not want to go home. She shook her head.

The nun wrote, "Parents not living." Grey-Eyes felt relieved.

There were two more times in the dining room. Twice more she had to eat what she did not like and did not want. She was surprised when Grey-Eyes told her that every day they ate three times. "Here we eat by clock time, not by stomach time," Grey-Eyes said. "You will learn to like the food and to like eating when you are not hungry." Tall-Girl doubted this.

At last the long day was ended with another time at church. This was called night prayers. Tall-Girl liked it. She liked the quiet and the peace of church. She was tired. Her head ached. Her back ached. Her heart ached. Although she would never have admitted it, she was homesick. She longed for the smell of the campfire and the sheep in the night corral.

They marched in line to the dormitory. Tall-Girl tried not to see that the door they entered faced the west. She tried not to see the windows in the north wall.

When the other girls lined up to take their showers, she stood quietly in the place that had been assigned to her. Always before this a bath had been a holy time, prepared for with fasting and prayer. When the other girls brushed their hair, standing before their small mirrors, she brushed hers, but she shut her eyes while she brushed it. Only witch-people brushed their hair at night. She did not see her reflection in the mirror. Her eyes were closed. She brushed her long hair with even, steady strokes. If there were things she must do in order to learn all that she must know for The People's good, she would do them.

She watched the other girls climb into the high narrow beds. She climbed into hers. Soon the lights went out. Blessed darkness filled the dormitory. Blessed quiet filled it. The other girls were asleep. Quietly she slipped out of bed, took her blanket from the locker. Then, wrapping it tightly around her, she went to sleep on the floor.

She dreamed, she dreamed that the wind talked with her, saying softly, saying gently: "Two things . . . two things . . . one to be given to you . . . one to be taken from you . . . ."

Tall-Girl stirred restlessly, still dreaming. She whispered, "This thing that will be given to me . . . I think I know what it is to be . . . . At least, I know what I want it to be."

"Two things . . . two things," the wind sighed softly.

"Two things?" Tall-Girl asked. "What is this other thing that is to be taken from me?"

Again the wind spoke softly, softly, a word lost almost as it was spoken. Tall-Girl's eyes opened. She looked into the dark heart of the night. "Fear?" she asked. "Wind, did you tell me 'Fear'?" She must be mistaken, she thought. Not fear. Not to her. Not to Chanter's Daughter who was not afraid to ride alone across an empty land, to face the storm, to brave a brown bear's den. She must have been mistaken.

The wind did not answer. It was silent. The dream was finished.

Finally Tall-Girl slept again and her heart felt comforted. In this strange place, the wind had found her. It had spoken to her. She was still a Daughter of The People. When the time was right, she would return to them and to their ways.

"No one sings the sunrise song," Tall-Girl said from her bed, calling over to Grey-Eyes who was still sleeping. She had been awake for a long time, having crawled back into bed where she was supposed to be. She felt refreshed. She had slept well, and only the comfort of her dream remained with her.

The morning warning bell sounded. Slowly the girls came awake. On their way to church, Tall-Girl said to Grey-Eyes, who was marching in front of her, "No one sings the sunrise song. I listened." Grey-Eyes looked around to see where Sister was. They were not supposed to talk in line. They were not supposed to speak Navajo, only for translation. Sister was at the back of the line.

Grey-Eyes spoke quickly. "Why should anyone sing the sunrise song here?" she asked.

"It's the way to begin the new day," Tall-Girl answered. "Why should these people here begin their day without a sunrise song?"

Grey-Eyes looked around again to see if Sister was in hearing distance. "Why?" she retorted. "Because they are not Navajo. That's why." Then she added crossly, "It's too bad you did not learn the English before you came here."

Tall-Girl was offended. She made no reply.

Grey-Eyes added, "Gentle-Sister has been teaching me for years, while you were with Chanter learning his ways."

Grey-Eyes felt better. If she were caught whispering in line, it would mean a demerit. She knew what demerits were. She did not like them.

The line of girls marched into the church. Tall-Girl pulled her blanket high around her head. She was still displeased. She saw and heard nothing.

At breakfast she was hungry. She ate, the food tasted good, and she felt better. She smiled at Grey-Eyes to show her she was forgiven. Grey-Eyes had forgotten that there was anything to forgive. She smiled back happily. The day began in peace.

Sister Jean Catherine met them. "Take your cousin to the hospital," she told Grey-Eyes, "and be sure you translate every word, just like you do for me."

Tall-Girl had heard the word hospital before. She remembered it. It was the place where Gentle-Sister had taken her little son. It was where all footprints of evil had been taken from his face. "The great Medicine Man who gave the Sing, he will be there, perhaps." Grey-Eyes looked her surprise. Tall-Girl said, by way of explanation, "The Sing for Gentle-Sister's baby that took the evil from him."

"Ah-h," Grey-Eyes thought, "she is here to learn his magic. She would add it to that which Chanter has given her." Aloud she said, "You mean the one who is called Doctor. Yes, he is at the hospital."

The two girls walked to the hospital. Inside the building, Tall-Girl felt as if she had stepped into a mid-winter world. Everything was white, white, white—long white dress, white shoes, white shawl-covering on the head. One of the Sister-clan asked questions; Grey-Eyes translated. Tall-Girl answered and did what she was told to do.

"She says, what's your name?"

"Despah Tseghi."

"She says, how old are you?"

"How old?"

"How many years do you have?"

"I don't know."

Grey-Eyes said, "Fifteen years, the same as I have." She added under her breath, "I think."

The translating went on and on. "She says, open your mouth." "She says show your teeth." "She says, say 'Aaah.'" Eyes, ears, throat, heart, lungs—the nurse was thorough. Despah was bewildered and exhausted. At last the nun said, "That will be all for now."

Grey-Eyes said, "She says to go. Come back tomorrow."

Tall-Girl was not ready to go. "I want to see the Medicine Man."

Grey-Eyes did not know what to say. New girls, even old girls, did not ask to see the Doctor. She did not answer.

The nun asked, "What does Despah want?"

Grey-Eyes answered the Sister, "I don't know." She said to Tall-Girl, "She says, wait until you get sick."

Tall-Girl was not satisfied. This was the place she wanted to be. She wanted to tell the white Medicine Man, "I am ready. I can learn what you have to teach me." Grey-Eyes walked out the door. Tall-Girl reluctantly followed her.

Grey-Eyes tried to explain. "Here at this place you sleep, you eat, you wear the clothes they give you, you learn what they teach you in the books, and you learn how to work." Grey-Eyes looked briefly at Tall-Girl. She wondered if her cousin were listening to what she said. Perhaps she was. She continued talking. "You get different books when you learn more English. It is this way also with the work. Only ones who know much English can work in the hospital place." In case Tall-Girl was listening, Grey-Eyes said, "Even I with all my English am not allowed to work there yet."

The girls walked on in silence. Grey-Eyes dreaded the next place she had been told to take her cousin. She dreaded what would happen when Sister Matilda took Tall-Girl's three calico skirts, her velvet blouse and her moccasins away from her. Tall-Girl could have them to wear when she went home again. She could not wear them here. Girls who went to St. Mary's wore the uniform. It was as Grey-Eyes had feared it would be, but at last it was over.

Tall-Girl's hair was still long. She would not let them cut it. She still wore the squash-blossom necklace. She would not let them keep it for her. Furiously she took the eagle feather from her moccasin and put it in the sole of her new shoes. It was her good luck omen. She would need it, she told Grey-Eyes to tell Sister Matilda, to get from this place what she had come to get. Grey-Eyes translated, "Her mother gave it to her. Please may she keep it?"

Sister Matilda was touched. "Of course," she said with understanding sympathy.

The next stop was at Sister Agnes' work-detail room. Sister Agnes was firm and business-like. "I'll put her with the knitting detail. We need a lot of sweaters knitted for this winter." Grey-Eyes' voice was timid and tired as she translated this to Tall-Girl, standing disdainful and proud in the shameful short skirt they had put on her.

When Grey-Eyes told her what her work-detail would be, she could not believe she had heard correctly. "Knitting!" she said. "Knitting! Knitting is man's work. Navajo men are the ones who knit the stockings for their families."

Grey-Eyes said, "Not here. Women and girls do the knitting here. At this place the men chop the wood. That is the way the ones who are in this place divide the work."

Tall-Girl closed her eyes. She heard the voice of Gentle-Sister saying, "A Sing is not enough. There must be more." She heard her own heart whispering, "Two things . . . two things . . . . You can find them here." She said aloud, "For my People's good." Then, turning to Grey-Eyes, "Tell her I will knit. If women here do men's work, I will do it."

Grey-Eyes did not bother to translate. Sister Agnes had not asked if the new girl would knit. She had said the new girl would knit. Sister Agnes did not know that Tall-Girl was Chanter's daughter. Grey-Eyes turned away. There was only one more place to take her cousin and she was glad. It had been a hard two days.

She said, "Now I take you to the place they call classroom. It is where they keep their books. Sister Jean Catherine is the teacher."

Tall-Girl said, "I thought you told me that one was the Clan Headsman."

"There are not enough Sisters here. All of them have two jobs." Grey-Eyes spoke shortly. "Too many new girls, not enough Sisters." She knocked loudly on the classroom door.

Tall-Girl shrugged her shoulders. It was all right with her if the one they called Grey-Eyes wanted to be a witch person. Everyone knew that only witches knocked on doors.

When the two girls entered the room, the nun pointed with her chin to an empty seat for Tall-Girl to take. Grey-Eyes told her, "I go now because I am in a better grade. I know the English."

Tall-Girl looked around the room. It was full, for the most part, of younger girls, those who were beginning English speech. Tall-Girl felt no shame that she was older and taller than the other girls. It did not occur to her that this could seem to be important. There were other things of far greater importance. The classroom door faced the east. There were no doors or windows in the north wall, only a black board with white marks on it. The classroom windows were at the west and south. Besides these good things that she noticed in the classroom, the one they called Sister Jean Catherine had pointed in the Navajo way, not with her finger and outstretched hand, but with her chin and lips. This was a good sign. Everything in the room was good. Her heart sang, "There is beauty around me." Her dark eyes turned to the nun who was to be her teacher with happy expectancy.

Winter closed in. Snow fell in lazily-swirling snowflakes of many shapes sprinkled with the shining dust of stars. Tall-Girl looked at the snowflakes sticking to the classroom window. Snow had never seemed beautiful to her before. It was something to be thankful for because it brought stored water to the thirsty lands in summer time. It was something to be dreaded and feared because of the suffering and harm it could bring to the flocks. It was something to be endured by The People as they huddled in their snow-banked hogans or plodded through the drifts to the sheep corral and the Trading Post.

But here it was beautiful. It softened the harsh lines of the empty land. It piled in thick softness on the steep, angular roofs of the school buildings. It drifted around the sharp, angular corners. It covered the ground in smooth unbroken whiteness.

Standing in a dry, warm classroom, looking out at the drifting feathers of the snow clouds, was a delight and a beauty. Tall-Girl's heart beat faster.

There was something else that the snow-filled winter brought to

St. Mary's. It brought a feeling of closeness, of warm security, of bright companionship among the girls and between them and the nuns who taught them. This was a new experience for Tall-Girl. Since she could remember she was of The People, dedicated to their good, but apart from them. She was Chanter's Daughter, which gave her a holiness, a power, a distinction, but barred her from the small intimacies of the everyday world. She had never been a girl with the other girls, a person with the people. She had been one who was being trained in the Holy Way.

But winter shut her in with the small secrets, and the little laughters of the other girls. Day by day she moved a little closer to the heart of this circle. She learned to unbend. She learned to be gay. She had always been beautiful, but now added to the beauty was a new, warm loveliness.

Exploring the Ideas

the setting

Based on the passage, indicate which are accurate and which are inaccurate statements about St. Mary's Mission. Then revise the inaccurate statements so they are correct.

1. One sister or nun is in charge of the school.
2. The school is five years old.
3. Church bells indicate that it is time to attend Mass.
4. During the religious service organ music is played.
5. The girls eat at different times.
6. The girls attend church only in the morning.
7. The girls could use Navajo only for translation.
8. The girls could talk to each other on their way to church.
9. At the school each girl is taught a particular skill.
10. Girls are assigned a class on the basis of their age.

characterization

In this selection the author frequently tells the reader directly how Tall-Girl felt. Match each of the feelings listed below with the time when Tall-Girl felt that way in the story. For each one indicate why you think she felt that way.

Feeling

1. Tall-Girl was shocked.
2. She was surprised.
3. She was pleased by this person's actions.
4. She was delighted.
5. She felt confused and faint.
6. She was embarrassed and felt ill at ease.
7. She could not believe what she heard.
8. She felt as if she had stepped into a mid-winter world.

Event

a. Tall-Girl attended Mass.
b. Grey-Eyes hugged her.
c. She heard the church bells.
d. Grey-Eyes was wearing a shortskirt and white blouse.
e. She was told to knit.
f. Sister Jean Catherine touched her fingertips in the Navajo way.
g. She stepped inside the hospital.
h. She ate for the first time in the dining hall.

the theme

LANGUAGE DIFFERENCES. Tall-Girl knows no English. Thus, she has to depend on Grey-Eyes to translate for her. The author describes several occasions when Grey-Eyes translates for her. For each occurrence indicate if Grey-Eyes' translation is accurate or inaccurate.

1. Sister Jean Catherine welcomes Tall-Girl.
2. Sister Jean Catherine tells her they are going to Mass.
3. Sister Angelica asks her name.
4. Sister Angelica asks if her parents are living.
5. The sister at the hospital asks her name and age.
6. Tall-Girl says she doesn't know her age.
7. The sister at the hospital tells Tall-Girl to open her mouth and show her teeth.
8. The sister at the hospital tells her that will be all.
9. Tall-Girl asks to see the Medicine Man.
10. The sister at the hospital asks what Tall-Girl wants.
11. Tall-Girl says she needs her eagle feather because it is a good luck omen.
12. Tall-Girl says she will knit.

Have you ever acted as a translator? Have you ever translated something inaccurately? Why did you do so? Why do you think Grey-Eyes sometimes translates incorrectly?

CULTURAL DIFFERENCES. Many things in the Mission School seem strange to Tall-Girl. For each of the following customs describe what is done at St. Mary's Mission School and what is typical for the Navajos.

Example

The common hair style for young girls
St. Mary's School: a short square bob
Navajos: long hair

1. The common dress for young girls
2. The method of pointing to something
3. The method of announcing the sunrise
4. The typical shape of buildings
5. The place where people eat
6. The company that people have when they eat
7. The time that people eat
8. The location of doors and windows
9. The manner of bathing
10. The time for brushing hair
11. Who typically knits in the society
12. Who knocks at doors

Exploring the Language

descriptive language

The author of *Medicine Man's Daughter* makes descriptions more vivid by comparing one item with another. Notice the following examples.

1. The walls of the dormitory "were full of windows like ghost eyes, vacant and sightless."
   How are the windows like ghost eyes?
2. In the hospital Tall-Girl "felt as if she had stepped into a mid-winter world."
   How is the hospital like winter?
3. "Snow fell in lazily-swirling snowflakes of many shapes sprinkled with the shining dust of stars."
   How are snowflakes like stars?

4. "Standing in a dry, warm classroom, looking out at the drifting feathers of the snow clouds, was a delight and a beauty."
   How might snow clouds be like drifting feathers?
5. What is being explained in the following sentence?
   "Sun-Carrier with the great sun in his arms had just begun the morning walk across the roof of the world."

Composing

comparing/contrasting

Compare and contrast typical customs of the Navajos and the white man as they are demonstrated at St. Mary's School. Begin by categorizing these customs into groups such as dress patterns or eating habits, and then compare and contrast the two cultures. You might organize the essay by discussing all of the customs of the Navajos before dealing with St. Mary's School, or you might deal first with the dress patterns of each, for example, and then proceed to a second topic.

photo: © Michal Heron 1982.

"A SONG FOR A BARBARIAN REED PIPE"

Maxine Hong Kingston

In this chapter from her autobiography, Maxine Hong Kingston refers to herself as "I," rather than in the third person, used earlier by the author in "At the Western Palace." Perhaps she uses the conventional pronoun because she is telling about a wholly American experience, going to kindergarten.

WHEN I WENT TO KINDERGARTEN and had to speak English for the first time, I became silent. A dumbness—a shame—still cracks my voice in two, even when I want to say "hello" casually, or ask an easy question in front of the check-out counter, or ask directions of a bus driver. I stand frozen, or I hold up the line with the complete, grammatical sentence that comes squeaking out at impossible length. "What did you say?" says the cab driver, or "Speak up," so I have to perform again, only weaker the second time. A telephone call makes my throat bleed and takes up that day's courage. It spoils my day with self-disgust when I hear my broken voice come skittering out into the open. It makes people wince to hear it. I'm getting better, though. Recently I asked the postman for special-issue stamps; I've waited since childhood for postmen to give me some of their own accord. I am making progress, a little every day.

My silence was thickest—total—during the three years that I covered my school paintings with black paint. I painted layers of black over houses and flowers and suns, and when I drew on the blackboard, I put a layer of chalk on top. I was making a stage curtain, and it was the moment before the curtain parted or rose. The teachers called my parents to school, and I saw they had been saving my pictures, curling and cracking, all alike and black. The teachers pointed to the pictures and looked serious, talked seriously too, but my parents did not understand English. ("The parents and teachers of criminals were executed," said my father.) My parents took the pictures home. I spread them out (so black and full of possibilities) and pretended the curtains were swinging open, flying up, one after another, sunlight underneath, mighty operas.

During the first silent year I spoke to no one at school, did not ask before going to the lavatory, and flunked kindergarten. My sister also said nothing for three years, silent in the playground and silent at lunch. There were other quiet Chinese girls not of our family, but most of them got over it sooner than we did. I enjoyed the silence. At first it did not occur to me I was supposed to talk or to pass kindergarten. I talked at home and to one or two of the Chinese kids in class. I made motions and even made some jokes. I drank out of a toy saucer when the water spilled out of the cup, and everybody laughed, pointing at me, so I did it some more. I didn't know that Americans don't drink out of saucers.

I liked the Negro students (Black Ghosts) best because they laughed the loudest and talked to me as if I were a daring talker too. One of the Negro girls had her mother coil braids over her ears Shanghai-style like mine; we were Shanghai twins except that she was covered with black like my paintings. Two Negro kids enrolled in Chinese school, and the teachers gave them Chinese names. Some Negro kids walked me to school and home, protecting me from the Japanese kids, who hit me and chased me and stuck gum in my ears. The Japanese kids were noisy and tough. They appeared one day in kindergarten, released from concentration camp, which was a tick-tac-toe mark, like barbed wire, on the map.

It was when I found out I had to talk that school became a misery, that the silence became a misery. I did not speak and felt bad each time that I did not speak. I read aloud in first grade, though, and heard the barest whisper with little squeaks come out of my throat. "Louder," said the teacher, who scared the voice away again. The other Chinese girls did not talk either, so I knew the silence had to do with being a Chinese girl.

Reading out loud was easier than speaking because we did not have to make up what to say, but I stopped often, and the teacher would think I'd gone quiet again. I could not understand "I." The Chinese "I" has seven strokes, intricacies. How could the American "I," assuredly wearing a hat like the Chinese, have only three strokes, the middle so straight? Was it out of politeness that this writer left off strokes the way a Chinese has to write her own name small and crooked? No, it was not politeness; "I" is a capital and "you" is lower-case. I stared at that middle line and waited so long for its black center to resolve into tight strokes and dots that I forgot to pronounce it. The other troublesome word was "here," no strong consonant to hang on to, and so flat, when "here" is two mountainous ideographs. The teacher, who had already told me every day how to read "I" and "here," put me in the low corner under the stairs again, where the noisy boys usually sat.

When my second grade class did a play, the whole class went to the auditorium except the Chinese girls. The teacher, lovely and Hawaiian, should have understood about us, but instead left us behind in the classroom. Our voices were too soft or nonexistent, and our parents never signed the permission slips anyway. They never signed anything unnecessary. We opened the door a crack and peeked out, but closed it again quickly. One of us (not me) won every spelling bee, though.

I remember telling the Hawaiian teacher, "We Chinese can't sing 'land where our fathers died.' " She argued with me about politics, while I meant because of curses. But how can I have that memory when I couldn't talk? My mother says that we, like the ghosts, have no memories.

After American school, we picked up our cigar boxes, in which we had arranged books, brushes, and an inkbox neatly, and went to Chinese school, from 5:00 to 7:30 P.M. There we chanted together, voices rising and falling, loud and soft, some boys shouting, everybody reading together, reciting together and not alone with one voice. When we had a memorization test, the teacher let each of us come to his desk and say the lesson to him privately, while the rest of the class practiced copying or tracing. Most of the teachers were men. The boys who were so well behaved in the American school played tricks on them and talked back to them. The girls were not mute. They screamed and yelled during recess, when there were no rules; they had fist fights. Nobody was afraid of children hurting themselves or of children hurting school property. The glass doors to the red and green balconies with the gold joy symbols were left wide open so that we could run out and climb the fire escapes. We played capture-the-flag in the auditorium, where Sun Yat-sen and Chiang Kai-shek's pictures hung at the back of the stage, the Chinese flag on their left and the American flag on their right. We climbed the teak ceremonial chairs and made flying leaps off the stage. One flag headquarters was behind the glass door and the other on stage right. Our feet drummed on the hollow stage. During recess the teachers locked themselves up in their office with the shelves of books, copybooks, inks from China. They drank tea and warmed their hands at a stove. There was no play supervision. At recess we had the school to ourselves, and also we could roam as far as we could go—downtown, Chinatown stores, home—as long as we returned before the bell rang.

At exactly 7:30 the teacher again picked up the brass bell that sat on his desk and swung it over our heads, while we charged down the stairs, our cheering magnified in the stairwell. Nobody had to line up.

Not all of the children who were silent at American school found voice at Chinese school. One new teacher said each of us had to get up and recite in front of the class, who was to listen. My sister and I had memorized the lesson perfectly. We said it to each other at home, one chanting, one listening. The teacher called on my sister to recite first. It was the first time a teacher had called on the second-born to go first. My sister was scared. She glanced at me and looked away; I looked down at my desk. I hoped that she could do it because if she could, then I would have to. She opened her mouth and a voice came out that wasn't a whisper, but it wasn't a proper voice either. I hoped that she would not cry, fear breaking up her voice like twigs underfoot. She sounded as if she were trying to sing though weeping and strangling. She did not pause or stop to end the embarrassment. She kept going until she said the last word, and then she sat down. When it was my turn, the same voice came out, a crippled animal running on broken legs. You could hear splinters in my voice, bones rubbing jagged against one another. I was loud, though. I was glad I didn't whisper. There was one little girl who whispered.

You can't entrust your voice to the Chinese, either; they want to capture your voice for their own use. They want to fix up your tongue to speak for them. "How much less can you sell it for?" we have to say. Talk the Sales Ghosts down. Make them take a loss.

Exploring the Ideas

the plot

In this passage from *The Woman Warrior* Maxine Hong Kingston relates several of her experiences in elementary school. She describes specific things that occurred during kindergarten, first grade, and second grade. Indicate when each of the following events occurred—in kindergarten, first grade, or second grade. If the event occurred during more than one year, use kindergarten through second grade. It may not always be clear from the story when the event occurred.

Example

Event: The author had to speak English for the first time
Time: kindergarten

1. She covered her school paintings with black.
2. The teacher called her parents to the school.
3. She spoke to no one at school.
4. She drank out of a toy saucer.
5. She read out loud.
6. The author did not take part in the class play.
7. She went to the Chinese school in the evening.

the characters

Which of the following adjectives do you think best describe the author during her early school years?

afraid	frustrated	shy
brave	happy	stubborn
confused	lonely	unhappy

Give several facts from the story that support your opinion about how the author felt while she was attending school.

The following questions may help you decide how Ms. Kingston felt at the American school.

1. Why does the author say she painted her pictures black?
2. Why do you think the author was silent at the American school but not at the Chinese school?
3. Why do you think she continued to drink out of a saucer even though everyone laughed at her?
4. Why do you think she liked having the Negro students talk to her as if she were a daring talker?

the theme

In which of the following situations do you usually use your native language? In which do you usually use English? Some of them may not apply to you.

1. at home with your parents
2. at home with your brothers and sisters
3. at your job with your co-workers
4. at church or in the community with older people
5. at church or in the community with people your age
6. with your girlfriend or boyfriend
7. with your husband or wife
8. when you're angry
9. when you're explaining something that is complicated
10. when you count or do math problems
11. when you're talking about food or cooking equipment

Describe three other occasions when you usually use your native language.

Which of following adjectives best describe how you usually feel when you use your native language? Which adjectives best describe how you usually feel when you use English?

confident	relaxed	talkative
frustrated	secure	timid
insecure	stupid	uneasy
intelligent		

symbolism

Below is a drawing of the Chinese character for the pronoun, I.

Why does the author think the symbol for "I" in English is unusual? What does she think it resembles? Did the author say "I" in English easily and naturally?

The author says that "here" sounds strange to her because it is so different from the Chinese word. Do you think that Maxine Hong Kingston felt at home here in the United States?

Are there any words in English that sound strange to you?

Exploring the Language

connecting devices

Connecting words of time such as *before, after, when, while, during,* and *at* are often used to indicate when something occurred. Maxine Hong Kingston uses many of these words to indicate when the events in the story occurred. For each of the following incidents, reread the text to find out exactly when they occurred. Then tell when the event occurred and which connecting word is used in the text to indicate the time it happened.

Example

Event: The author became silent.
Connecting devices: when
Time: She went to kindergarten and had to speak English.

1. Her silence was the thickest.
2. She spoke to no one at school.
3. School was a misery.
4. Everyone except the Chinese girls went to the auditorium.
5. She went to the Chinese school.
6. The students went up to the teacher's desk.
7. The students screamed and yelled.
8. The teachers locked themselves up in their offices.
9. The children had the school to themselves.
10. The teacher picked up the brass bell.

descriptive language

Maxine Hong Kingston lets her readers know just how painful it was for her to speak in school several times. For instance, she says, "a dumbness—a shame—still cracks my voice in two." A voice, of course, is not literally a solid object that can be cracked in two, though the vocal chords that produce the sound are concrete things. Yet a voice can sound as if it had been broken in two. Can you make such a sound? How did it feel to try? How did you react to hearing someone else make it?

When she says a telephone call makes her throat bleed, do you think her throat is literally bleeding? Why do you think she says it bleeds rather than says "tighten" or "dry up"?

During her sister's recitation in Chinese school, Maxine hoped her sister would not cry, "fear breaking up her voice like twigs underfoot." Why do you think Maxine didn't want her sister to cry? Under what conditions could you hear twigs breaking underfoot? What would be likely to cause them to break?

Her own voice came out "a crippled animal running on broken legs. You could hear splinters in my voice, bones rubbing jagged against one another." What words tell you how painful it was for her to speak? Why do you think she calls her voice an animal?

Maxine Hong Kingston calls the chapter from which this passage has been excerpted, "A Song for a Barbarian Reed Pipe." (A reed pipe is a musical instrument made out of the hollow stems of grass.) What sort of song would a voice like hers sing? Which is barbaric, or uncivilized, in her description: the Chinese school or the American school?

Composing

comparing/contrasting

Both *Medicine Man's Daughter* and "A Song for a Barbarian Reed Pipe" deal with the theme of adjusting to school in a foreign setting. In order to explore the similarities and differences between the situations, refer to the selections to find what each story says about the following points. For numbers 3, 4, and 5, cite specific examples from the text that illustrate your conclusion.

Example

Type of school that the central character attended
Medicine Man's Daughter: A private school where the students lived
"A Song for a Barbarian Reed Pipe": A public school

1. The age of the central character at the time of the story
2. The central character's knowledge of English
3. The central character's attitude toward school
4. The central character's willingness to do what she is told
5. Which things the central character finds strange in the new culture

Compare and contrast the ways in which the central character in "A Song for a Barbarian Reed Pipe" and *Medicine Man's Daughter* adjust to school in a strange setting. One way to organize the essay is to discuss Maxine Hong Kingston's adjustment in terms of such things as her proficiency in English and her willingness to cooperate in school and then to compare and contrast these same aspects in regard to Tall-Girl. A second possibility is to deal with topics such as willingness to cooperate in school, discussing both characters and then to deal with another topic, such as proficiency in English.

photo: Arthur Rothstein.

from BARRIO BOY

Ernesto Galarza

From *Barrio Boy*, by Ernesto Galarza, 1971. Reprinted by permission of University of Notre Dame Press.

Ernesto Galarza was born in 1905. As a young boy, he and his family came from Mexico to live in Sacramento, California. He describes his exploration of his new neighborhood in this excerpt from his autobiography.

EXCEPT FOR OURSELVES, THE TENANTS OF 418 L were far from being a family; they were more like a collection. There was something peculiar about each one; they were people who stayed out of each other's way but who didn't mind being noticed and who noticed you. I went for Mr. Howard's laundry and he loaned me a book called *Enoch Arden*. The Old Gentleman knocked on our wall when he was ready to put on his necktie and coat, a signal for me to go and help him. Every now and then he pressed a dime into my hand or bought me a chocolate bar when I walked with him to the corner and back. My mother helped the Indian lady with her wash, and she took me to the State Fair one summer where she bought me a whip and a cowboy belt. Tenants came and went but the familiar characters like us, stayed on. From them my circle of acquaintances and friends began to spread around the block.

One of the first of these was Big Singh, the brawny Hindu who ran a boarding house next door for his fellow countrymen. Big Singh with his thick black beard always wore a dark turban wound around his head and a white apron from his neck to his ankles. His side porch looked over our yard and Big Singh would lean on the railing chatting with us in the few English words he knew. I became Big Singh's tutor, for he often asked me how to say certain words in English, which I supplied with complete confidence. As a show of appreciation he hired me to work in his kitchen on Saturday afternoons to turn over the thick flour cakes he prepared for his boarders and which he called ruti. On weekends many of the Sikh laborers came there to eat and sleep. They were all enormous, like Big Singh, and all wore beards and turbans of different colors.

Up the street from us, toward Fourth, there was Miss Florence who lived in a second story flat and accompanied herself on the piano. She sang, very loudly, a song called "I want Sympathy," swooping up and down the bars melodiously like someone on a long, high swing. She beat rugs on her front porch and called out to me when she saw me pass by. Her rugged, unlovely face broke into smiles when I called back, as I always did, "Miss Florence, sing Sympathy."

Around the block, on the alley corner, there was Stacy's blacksmith shop, a small barn shaded by one of the soaring elms that made the street look like the inside of a cathedral. Stacy, a square-jawed strongman, allowed boys to stand in the wide doorway while he fitted iron shoes to the horses. When business was good, the customers lined up in the alley or the street, tied to the elm and the hitching posts. Stacy pumped the bellows of his forge with gusto, making the flames leap around the shoe he was shaping. He laid it red hot on the anvil and whammed it with his hammer, which he rested loosely so that it danced and tinkled after each blow. The hot shoe was dunked in a barrel of water and Stacy, rubbing one huge hand down the horse's withers pulled up the hoof, clamped it between his knees, and proceeded to secure it with the nails he held pressed between his lips. Stacy was a comedian and when we were watching he invented bits of funny business for us. One of these was to place an empty pail under a horse which decided to let go with his water while he was being shod. Stacy would offer us the bucket with a flourish and an invitation to "have a drink on the house." It was our cue to take the bucket and empty it in the gutter.

Behind Stacy's there was a Chinese hand laundry and above that a rickety loft where boxers trained. In all the years I did business with the laundryman as errand boy for some of his customers, we never said a word to each other; but when a boxer was tapping off a furious rhythm on the punching bag above us, shaking the building, the laundryman and I listened together. That, and a quick nod when he matched my ticket with a package of laundry, was the extent of our communication.

Halfway down the alley lived a Yugoslav who worked in the railroad shops and ran a bowling alley. It was a dirt strip, tamped down, with a border of planks. On Sundays the Slavs gathered to play bocce, and once a year the alley was covered with boards and turned into a winery. A large press was brought out of the cellar, and the men, chattering and drinking, pressed the grapes with their bare feet, their pants rolled up above the knees. They offered me nips of wine and lowered me into the press to tramp grapes myself.

At the Fourth Street end of the alley there was a fish shop run by a Japanese who sometimes bought from me the catfish I caught in the river. We never argued about the price. As with the laundryman, ours was a speechless acquaintance, my fish and his nickels crossing the counter in opposite directions, without a word being said.

This was our alley, along with the shanties, the barns, and the sagging cottages behind picket or plank fences. It was a refuge for sleeping drunks, and I often passed by them looking for gunnysacks, beer bottles, and scraps of tinfoil.

Exploring the Ideas

the characters

In the passage Ernesto Galarza describes the people of his neighborhood. For each of the following people give anything you are told about the character (his or her age, dress, occupation, build, etc.), and anything you are told about the relationship of each with the author.

Notice that Galarza does not call some of them by name. Why do you think he does this? How does he identify them?

Example

The character: The Old Gentleman
Description: wore a coat and necktie
Relationship with the author: gave the author a dime or bought him a chocolate bar for walking with him to the corner

1. The Indian lady
2. Big Singh
3. Miss Florence
4. Stacy
5. The Chinese laundryman
6. The Yugoslav
7. The Japanese

the location

For each of the characters, indicate what you are told about where they live.

Example

The character: Mr. Howard
Location: lived right next door to Galarza

1. Big Singh
2. Miss Florence
3. Stacy
4. The Chinese laundryman

5. The Yugoslav
6. The Japanese

From what you have found, draw a map of where these people live in relation to Galarza.

Exploring the Language

descriptive language

Galarza uses several comparisons to describe the neighborhood and its people. For example, Galarza states that Miss Florence "sang, very loudly, a song called 'I want Sympathy,' swooping up and down the bars melodiously like someone on a long, high swing." How was her singing like someone on a swing? Later he states that the soaring elms by Stacy's barn made the street "look like the inside of a cathedral." What do soaring elms and the inside of a cathedral have in common?

vocabulary

In describing the work of the blacksmith, Galarza uses several words that are specific to this trade. Use the clues that follow to try to guess the meaning of the italicized word. The statements following the sentences illustrate how you can use context clues to guess the meaning of the italicized word.

1. "Stacy pumped the *bellows* of his *forge* with gusto, making the flames leap around the shoe he was shaping." (line 42)
   Oxygen is needed to make a fire burn. Pumping the *bellows* made the flame increase. So a *bellows* is a . . . .
   The *forge* contains hot flames. So a *forge* is a . . . .
2. Stacy laid the shoe "red hot on the anvil and whammed it with his hammer, which he rested loosely so that it danced and tinkled after each blow." (line 44)
   The metal shoe was placed on the *anvil* in order to hammer it. So an *anvil* is a . . . .
3. One of Stacy's jokes "was to place an empty pail under a horse which decided to let go with his water while he was being *shod*." (line 50)
   In this paragraph what process is the author describing? So *to be shod* is to . . . .

Composing

describing a place and the people

Describe your present neighborhood or a place where you have lived. As Galarza has done, tell what you know about your neighbors and describe your relationship with them. If you do not know their names, give them a name as Galarza has done. Be sure to also describe where these people live in relation to your house.

expressing opinions

Ernesto Galarza's neighborhood is composed of people from many different countries. Some immigrants, however, prefer to live in neighborhoods that include people mainly from their own country. Which type of neighborhood do you think provides a better environment for a newly arrived immigrant to learn to live in a different culture?

What advantages do immigrants have in living in the type of neighborhood described by Galarza? What disadvantages?

What advantages do they have in living in a neighborhood that is mainly composed of people from their own country? What disadvantages?

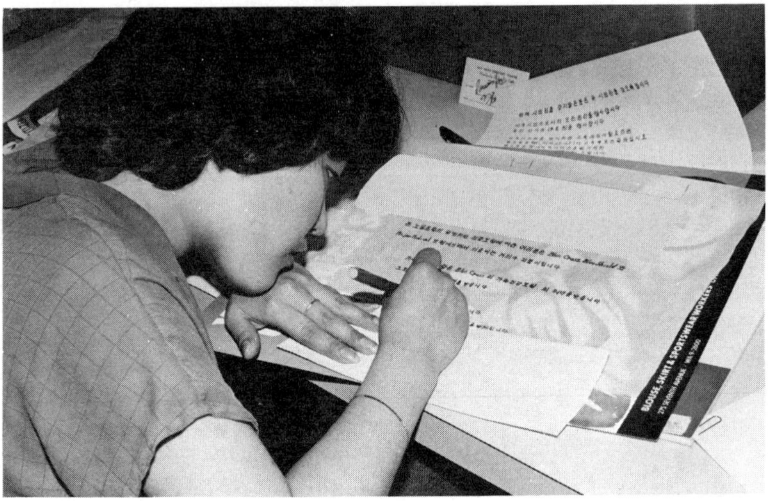

photo: Laimute E. Druskis.

from CHILD OF THE OWL

Laurence Yep

Child of the Owl is the story of a twelve-year-old girl named Casey whose mother, a Chinese-American, died when she was quite young. She lived with her father, Barney, until one day he was hospitalized. As a result, her father sent her to live with her maternal grandmother in the Chinatown district of San Francisco. Casey never learned to speak Chinese when she lived with her father. However, when she moved in with her grandmother, whom she called Paw-Paw, she was sent to a school in Chinatown that had an hour of instruction in Chinese each day. The following passage describes her experience in learning Chinese.

THE WORST THING OF ALL WAS CHINESE SCHOOL. I still get nightmares about it sometimes. I wasn't a bad student in the American school, but one hour out of each day the nuns left several classes and in would come the Chinese teachers. Right away they put me into the dummies' class, which met in an old room used to store old desks that were so old they had little holes with iron bottoms for putting ink bottles into. I found out quick enough that even this class was too tough for me. They taught school on the assumption that the kids already knew some Chinese, so they would explain the simple words in the textbooks with even simpler words—but I didn't even know those simple words.

The teacher was a plain-faced lady whose pancake makeup peeled in little patches so it looked like she had some kind of skin disease. She wore a sleeveless silk dress that hugged her body all the way down to her knees except for the slit that showed one leg.

On Monday the teacher stood in front of the class to read that week's lesson from the thin little paperback that was our textbook. The lesson had a colored picture of ants crawling over a rotton pomegranate and the teacher explained the picture and story with a lot of hand gestures. Then she started to read the story out loud again slowly, accenting each word carefully and pausing after each sentence, which ended in an American-style period. Then she waved at the class to repeat the line. No one else was having trouble reading the words but all I saw was a bunch of squiggly lines so I took out my pencil to copy down the sounds I heard. I did that for about five sentences and then I heard the teacher. "What are you doing?" She spoke as if her mouth were full of marbles when she tried to speak English.

"I'm trying to write down the sounds." I held up my book. "See?"

The teacher's eyebrows came together and she pursed her lips as if she were having trouble following me and wording her own answer. "That no good. You . . . you think too much 'Merican. Not think Chinese. Never learn. You erase."

"But how am I going to be able to read the words out loud if I don't know what they sound like?"

I heard the teacher tap her foot impatiently. Even if she had enough English to explain—and I wasn't sure about that—she didn't want to take the time for just one dumb student. I didn't have to know Chinese to see that she ran her class like it was some well-oiled machine. She was so used to a certain routine that she hated to break it. "You erase," she insisted.

"But how—"

"YOU ERASE." She snatched the book out of my hand and hit me with it. She didn't hit me hard enough to hurt, only to shock. Then she tossed my book back on top of my desk. "You 'Merican-born. Lazy, Lazy, Lazy." Then she folded her left arm over her stomach and holding up her book in her right hand, she began to walk back up the aisle, reading the next sentence in the lesson. I sat for a while, listening to all the crazy sounds, and then I picked up my pencil and slowly began to erase what I had written, leaving the page without any meaning to me.

On Tuesday we had calligraphy where we'd insert a pattern of basic words inside sheets of rice paper and copy the words in ink—it was a bit like painting, so at first I liked it till the teacher slapped my wrist with a ruler for holding the brush wrong and then, because my wrist hurt, I did the words sloppy and got an F.

On Wednesday we got to recite the lesson from memory. The others had no trouble because they at least knew what sounds the words were supposed to be. I memorized as much of the lesson as I was able to get sounds for but even that made the teacher mad because while I think I got the sounds right, I didn't know the tones. Every word in Chinese has a tone—like when your voice rises at the end of a question. I just threw in a tone wherever I wanted, so that at first the teacher winced and finally just hid her face in the textbook and told me to sit down.

Thursday we copied the lesson out on narrow rectangles of rice paper that were ruled off in red ink into squares. You wrote a word in each square—which was pretty easy. But Friday we had to write the lesson out from memory. It was easier for the other kids because it was a story to them, but to me the test meant I had to memorize a pattern of pictures. Still I did okay on that, getting every stroke in the right place. After I'd handed in my test, I sat back in my desk feeling pretty good. The teacher picked up her ballpoint pen and scanned over my test, frowning. Then she got up from her desk and came down the aisle. She clicked her pen shut and threw my test onto my desk. "How you do that? Not one word wrong."

"I learned the lesson," I said.

The teacher's lips moved silently, if she were trying to figure out the words for what she wanted to say next. "This too good. You copy book when I not looking."

"I didn't copy any book," I said indignantly. "I don't cheat."

"You not speak Chinese. You not read. You not even hold brush right. And you do this?" Her voice rose angrily. "You copy book."

"I've got a good memory. Want to see me do it again?"

"You know not enough time. Only five minutes left. You copy book."

"Are you calling me a liar?" I was getting just as mad as she was.

She wanted to go into a real tirade then. The whole class had stopped whatever they were doing, turning to watch us. But she knew that if she did it in Chinese, I wouldn't understand her, so it would be wasted. And yet her English wasn't good enough or she was just too mad to think. All she could say was "You too dumb. You copy book." She said each sound like it was exploding from her mouth. Then she clicked her pen point out and stabbed my test paper and scrawled out a big F across the surface. After that I just gave up trying.

The simplest thing would have been to go to Paw Paw and ask her to help me, but for one thing I never said I wanted to learn Chinese. I was an American and I couldn't see any good reason to learn a foreign language. And then, too, it hurts your pride when you think you're smart and you have to do things that make you feel dumb.

Exploring the Ideas

the characters

Choose which of the following adjectives you think best describe the teacher. Then point out things in the text that support your opinion.

cruel	organized
frustrated	short-tempered
impatient	strict
insecure	violent
insistent	unfair

Choose which of the following adjectives you think best describe Casey. Then point out things in the text that support your opinion.

aggressive	frustrated
conscientious	insecure
dumb	smart

In order to explore the relationship between the teacher and Casey state your opinion about the following matters. Be sure to give a reason to support your opinion.

1. Do you think the teacher should have hit Casey with a book when she wrote in it? Do you think the teacher should have slapped Casey's wrist for holding the brush incorrectly? In your native country do teachers ever hit their students? Do you think a teacher should ever hit a student? If so, describe a case when you think a teacher is justified in hitting a student.
2. Do you think the teacher should have called Casey lazy and dumb? What would you do if you had a student who you believed was lazy and dumb?
3. Do you think the teacher should have accused Casey of cheating? What would you do if you thought one of your students was cheating?
4. Why do you think the teacher treats Casey the way she does?
5. Why do you think Casey gave up trying to learn Chinese?

the theme

The excerpt illustrates many of the problems and frustrations involved in learning a second language. For example, when Casey can't read the characters she tries to write down the sounds she hears. Why do you think she does that? When you hear a word pronounced in English that you don't know, what do you do?

1. What strategy does Casey use to pass the test? Does she understand the lesson?
2. Have you ever done well on a test in English even though you weren't sure about the meaning of the words?
3. When you hear someone speaking your native language who doesn't know it well, how does that person sound to you? According to Casey, how does the teacher sound when she speaks English? What does the teacher do when Casey speaks Chinese and puts the tone in wherever she wants?
4. At the end of the passage Casey comments, "I was an American and I couldn't see any good reason to learn a foreign language."

Do you agree or disagree with her position? List three reasons to support your position.

Exploring the Language

The teacher, of course, does not speak English well. Rephrase the teacher's comments into standard English.

1. That no good.
2. You 'Merican-born.
3. You too dumb.
4. You not speak Chinese.
5. You not read.
6. You not even hold brush right.

What verbs did you add when you rewrote the sentences? Ask a native speaker of Chinese if the verb *to be* and the auxiliary *do* are used in Chinese. Why do you think the teacher makes the errors that she does?

Composing

comparing/contrasting

Both "A Song for a Barbarian Reed Pipe" and *Child of the Owl* describe a young girl's frustration in attending a school in which they are not fluent in the language. Yet there are many differences in the two selections. One obvious difference is that Maxine Hong Kingston is a Chinese-American who is trying to learn English, whereas Casey is a Chinese-American who is struggling to learn Chinese.

Write an essay in which you compare and contrast the experiences of the two main characters in these selections. You might consider the following questions.

What was the motivation of each character for learning a second language? How successful was each in learning this language?

In what ways was their background and personality the same or different?

How did they each express their frustration in learning a second language? Did other members of the class share their frustrations?

How did the teacher in each case help or hinder their learning the language?

photo: Jill Krementz.

OUT OF ORDER

William Saroyan

In Lilla Heston et al. (eds.), *The Search for Self* (Evanston, Ill.: McDougal, Littell and Company, 1972).

If this picture of William Saroyan could speak, would you expect him to tell a sad or a happy story? Would you expect him to take himself seriously or to make fun of himself?

LONGFELLOW HIGH WAS NOT STRICTLY SPEAKING A HIGH SCHOOL AT ALL. It was the seventh and eighth grades of grammar school, and its full name was Longfellow Junior High School. The Longfellow in question was of course *the* Mr. Longfellow, or Henry Wadsworth, although nothing much was ever made of that.

It was in ancient history that I first astonished my class into an awareness that here was a truly original mind. It happened that this was the first class of the very first day. The teacher was a hairy-faced, gray-and-brown looking woman of forty or so who was said to be, in spite of her offensive-looking skinny body and her drab clothes, fast. She smoked cigarettes, laughed loudly with other teachers during the lunch hour, and had frequently been seen by the older students running suddenly, pushing, and acting gay. She was called Miss Shenstone by the students and Harriet or Harry by the other teachers, excepting Miss Balthus, who called her Miss Shenstone and never permitted herself to be pushed. Ancient-history books were distributed to the class, and Miss Shenstone asked us to turn to page 192 for the first lesson.

I remarked that it would seem more in order to turn to page one for the first lesson.

I was asked my name, whereupon I was only too glad to say honestly, "William Saroyan."

"Well, William Saroyan," Miss Shenstone said, "I might say, *Mister* William Saroyan, just shut up and let me do the teaching of ancient history in this class."

Quite a blow.

On page 192, I recall quite clearly, was a photograph of two rather common-looking stones which Miss Shenstone said were called Stonehenge. She then said that these stones were twenty thousand years old.

It was at this point that my school of thought and behavior was started.

"How do you know?" I said.

This was a fresh twist to the old school: the school of thought in which the teachers asked the questions and the students tried to answer them. The entire class expressed its approval of the new school. There was a good deal of vocal enthusiasm. What happened might be accurately described as a demonstration. The truth of the matter is that neither Miss Shenstone, or Harry (as she enjoyed being called), nor Mr. Monsoon himself, the principal, had anything like a satisfactory answer to any legitimate question of this sort, for they (and all the other teachers) had always accepted what they had found in the textbooks.

Instead of trying to answer the question, Miss Shenstone compelled me to demonstrate the *behavior* of the new school. That is, she compelled me to run. She flung herself at me with such speed that I was scarcely able to get away. For half a moment she clung to my homeknit sweater, and damaged it before I got away. The class approved of the behavior of the new school also. Instead of remaining in one's seat in a crisis, it was better to get up and go. The chase was an exciting one, but I got out of the room safely. Five minutes later, believing that the woman had calmed down, I opened the door to step in and return to my seat, but again she flung herself at me, and again I got away.

Rather than wait for the consequences, I decided to present my case to Mr. Monsoon himself, but when I did so, I was amazed to find that his sympathies were with Miss Shenstone and that he looked upon me with loathing.

"She said the rocks were twenty thousand years old," I said. "All I said was, 'How do you know?' I didn't mean they *weren't* that old. I meant that maybe they were older, maybe thirty thousand years old. How old is the earth? Several million years old, isn't it? If the book can say the rocks are twenty thousand years old, somebody ought to be able to say how the book got that figure. This isn't Emerson School, it's Longfellow Junior High. I came here to learn. I don't expect to be punished because I want to learn."

"Your name again, please?" Mr. Monsoon said.

"William Saroyan," I said as humbly as possible, although I must confess it was not easy to do.

"You are?" Mr. Monsoon said.

"Eleven," I said.

"No, I don't mean that."

"One hundred and three pounds."

"No, no."

"Presbyterian."

"The *name*, I'm thinking of."

"It's said to mean blond."

"Nationality," Mr. Monsoon said.

"Armenian," I said proudly.

"Just as I thought," the principal said.

"Just as you thought *what*?"

"Nobody but an Armenian would have asked a question like that."

"How do you know?" I said, giving the new school another whirl.

"Nobody *did*," the principal said. "Does that answer your question?"

"Only partly," I said. "How do you know somebody else would *not* have asked it if I hadn't?"

"In all the years that I have been connected with the public school system of California," Mr. Monsoon said, "no one has ever asked such a question."

"Yes," I said quickly, "and in all the years before Newton wanted to know what made the apple fall, nobody wanted to know what made it fall."

At the time I believed that some day Mr. Monsoon would give an accurate account of this discussion, for I had no reason to believe he could not write or that he was not aware he was in the presence of a man it was his *duty* to remember. But there it is, the man never wrote such an account.

I was brilliant.

It's not my fault nobody else was.

Mr. Monsoon chose not to continue the discussion. He just sat and looked at his shoes.

"How about *that*?" I said.

"Well," he said rather wearily, "I must give you a thrashing. How about *that*?"

"For what?" I said.

I got to my feet, watching the stenographer, whose desk was beside the door. This was a rather pretty girl, and I had hoped to make a favorable impression on her, although I can't imagine what I expected to come of it.

"Miss Slifo," Mr. Monsoon said, but that was all I needed to hear, and before Miss Slifo was able to block my way, I was at the door, out of the room, and just about halfway across the school grounds.

Once again, the behavior of the new school had been tested and found true.

I went home and found my Uncle Alecksander, who was studying law at the University of Southern-California, on a visit at our house, drinking coffee in the parlor. I told him the story. He invited me into his Apperson convertible and we took off for Longfellow Junior High School.

"That's the story, just as you've told it to me?" he said as we rode.

"That's exactly how it happened."

"All right," my Uncle Alecksander said. "You wait in the car."

I don't know what my Uncle Alecksander and Mr. Monsoon said to one another, but after a few minutes Miss Slifo came out to the car and said, "Your uncle and Mr. Monsoon and Miss Shenstone would like to see you in the office."

I went in and my uncle said, "There are men who know how to determine the approximate age of different things in the world and on the earth. Who these men are and how they determine these things, Mr. Monsoon does not know, and neither does Miss Shenstone. Miss Shenstone has promised to look into the matter. On your part, you may ask any question you like, but in a more cooperative and polite tone of voice." He turned to the principal. "Is that in accordance with our understanding?"

"Quite," the principal said.

"It was with *admiration* that Mr. Monsoon remarked that only an Armenian would have asked a question like that," my Uncle Alecksander went on. "Is that correct, Mr. Monsoon?"

"It is," Mr. Monsoon said. "In a city with a population of ten or fifteen thousand of them, I could scarcely—"

"With admiration, then," my Uncle Alecksander said. He turned to me.

"You will spend the rest of this day away from school, but tomorrow you will return to your classes as though nothing had happened.

"Is *that* also in accordance with our understanding?" he asked the principal.

"I was wondering if he might not be transferred to Hawthorne," the principal said, but my uncle said quickly, "He lives in this district. His friends come to this school. I shall be interested in his progress."

"We *all* shall," the principal said.

I could not have been more ill at ease, or more angry at my uncle. The very thing I had always despised had just taken place, supposedly on my behalf: that is to say, a brilliant man had come to my defense, a circumstance I could hardly be expected to enjoy.

A brilliant man, who happened to be my mother's younger brother, had stepped in among the great figures of the school, belittled, bossed, and threatened them: and they, instead of fighting back, had meekly permitted him to get away with it. Well, I didn't *want* him to get away with it.

The following day I presented myself to Mr. Monsoon, who, when he saw me, appeared to want to close his eyes and go to sleep.

"I've come to apologize," I said. "I don't want any special privileges."

"Just ask your question in a polite tone of voice," the man said. "You may go now."

He refused to open his eyes.

I went straight to the ancient-history class, where I found Miss Shenstone at her desk, gravely at work.

"I'm sorry about the trouble I made," I said. "I won't do it again."

For an instant I thought she was about to fling herself at me again, but after a moment she seemed to sink inwardly quite a bit, and then, without looking up from her work, she said very dryly, "They have a way of determining such things. You may go now."

I felt sure the principal and the teacher would one day remember how handsomely I had behaved in this unfortunate affair, but as I've said, they didn't, and so I have *had* to.

As luck would have it, Miss Shenstone taught at Longfellow only another four days, and during that time did not permit herself to look at me once or to ask me a question. She even gave up calling the roll, for fear that in acknowledgment of my name I might have something to say. A series of substitute teachers took over the teaching of the ancient-history class, but by now the new school was in full operation throughout Longfellow High, and the substitutes were always eager to finish out a day or a week and be gone forever.

Mr. Monsoon spoke about manners at several student body meetings in the school auditorium, but nobody took the hint, and after a month he too left the school and was succeeded by a man who was famous for his daring exploits as a captain in the First World War. It was expected of this man to quickly put down the new school and to restore the old. He tried the method of brute force at first, thrashing as many as three dozen boys a day, and then he tried the method of taking the worst boys into his confidence, going for walks with them through the school grounds, being a pal, and so on: but neither of these methods worked, and after the first semester, the man accepted a post at a small country school with only forty or fifty students.

As for myself, I transferred to Tech High in order to learn typing.

Exploring the Ideas

the characters

The following sentences describe things that Miss Shenstone, Mr. Monsoon, the Uncle, and William Saroyan said or did. For each item, give an adjective that might be used to describe their behavior.

Example

Behavior: Miss Shenstone ". . . laughed loudly with other teachers during the lunch hour, and had frequently been seen by the older students running suddenly, pushing, and acting gay."
Adjective: immature, impulsive

Miss Shenstone

1. After William asked the question about the age of the stone, "she flung herself" at him. When he returned to class, she did the same thing again.
2. After the discussion with William's uncle, she agreed to look into finding out how the age of Stonehenge was determined.
3. After the incident occurred, Miss Shenstone no longer looked at William in class nor asked him any questions.
4. She quit Longfellow School four days after the incident.

You may find the following adjectives helpful in describing Miss Shenstone.

aggressive	cowardly	strange
apologetic	immature	upset
ashamed	improper	violent
childish	impulsive	weird
compromising	incompetent	wild
cooperative	scared	

If you were a teacher, what would you have done if William Saroyan had asked you about how the age of the stone was determined?

Mr. Monsoon

1. When William said that he was an Armenian, he said, "Nobody but an Armenian would have asked a question like that."
2. He told William that he must give him a thrashing.

3. After the discussion with the uncle, he said that he had meant to make the comment that only an Armenian would ask a question like that with admiration.
4. He suggested to the uncle that William might be transferred to another school.
5. A month after the incident, he left Longfellow School.

You may find the following adjectives helpful in describing Mr. Monsoon.

bigoted	forgiving	threatening
cowardly	prejudiced	unfair
diplomatic	reasonable	unforgiving
fair	strict	unreasonable

What would you have done if you were a principal and William Saroyan had come to you with an account of what happened in Miss Shenstone's class?

The Uncle

1. After hearing his nephew's story, he went to the school with him and talked with Mr. Monsoon and Miss Shenstone.
2. He related the agreement they all had reached.
3. He said that William should not be transferred to another school because he lived in this district and his friends went to this school.

You may find the following adjectives helpful in describing the uncle.

concerned	frank	protective
diplomatic	insistent	righteous
firm	principled	supportive

What would you have done if you were William Saroyan's uncle and he had come to you with an account of what had happened at school?

William Saroyan

1. In reference to the age of Stonehenge, William asked Miss Shenstone, "How do you know?"
2. He ran out of the room when Miss Shenstone flung herself at him.
3. He went to present his case to Mr. Monsoon himself.
4. He ran out of the principal's office when he was told he was going to get a thrashing.

5. He told Mr. Monsoon, "I came here to learn. I don't expect to be punished because I want to learn."
6. The day after his uncle talked with Mr. Monsoon and Miss Shenstone, he went in and apologized to them.

You may find the following adjectives helpful in describing William Saroyan.

aggressive	frank	proud
bold	honest	reasonable
brave	impolite	rebellious
cowardly	inquisitive	scared
curious	insistent	smart
determined	intelligent	straightforward
disrespectful	polite	wise
foolish		

As a student would you ever ask a teacher how they know that something is a fact?

the theme

What do you think Saroyan means by the *old school* and the *new school* in the following sentences?

"This was a fresh twist to the *old school:* the school of thought in which the teachers asked the questions and the students tried to answer them."
"Instead of trying to answer the question, Miss Shenstone compelled me to demonstrate the *behavior* of the *new school.*"

Which type of school do you think is better?

In the story William Saroyan gets in trouble because he breaks several accepted conventions of classroom behavior. Each of the following sentences describes something that he does which is not typically done in schools. Some of them also describe behavior that is unusual for a teacher or principal. For each one, indicate what you think is the accepted way to behave in American schools.

Example

Miss Shenstone tells William, ". . . just shut up and let me do the teaching of ancient history in this class."
Convention that is broken: This type of language is not considered

acceptable for teachers in a classroom. They might say a similar thing in a more polite manner.

1. Miss Shenstone asks the class to turn to page 192 in their history book for their first lesson. William remarks that it would seem more in order to start on page one for the first lesson.
   What convention does Miss Shenstone break?
   What convention does William break?
2. In reference to the age of Stonehenge, William asks, "How do you know?"
   What convention does William break?
3. William presents his own case to Mr. Monsoon before Miss Shenstone goes to him.
   What convention does William break?
4. When Mr. Monsoon says that only an Armenian would ask a question like that, William asks the principal how he knows someone else would not have asked the same question.
   What convention does Mr. Monsoon break?
   What convention does William break?
5. After the principal says that he must give William a thrashing William, asks, "For what?"
   What convention does William break?
6. William runs out of the office when he hears he is going to get a thrashing.
   What convention does William break?

Exploring the Language

author's attitude

The way a story is told reflects the author's attitude. In "Out of Order," as Saroyan is telling the story, he is also commenting on what happened. For each of the following statements, choose the words and phrases that show Saroyan's opinion about the incident and about himself as a seventh-grader.

1. "It was in ancient history that I first astonished my class into an awareness that here was a truly original mind."
2. He told Mr. Monsoon his name "as humbly as possible, although I must confess it was not easy to do."
3. After his discussion with Mr. Monsoon he thinks, "I was brilliant. It's not my fault nobody else was."

4. After the incident, he comments, "I felt sure the principal and the teacher would one day remember how handsomely I had behaved in this unfortunate affair, but as I've said, they didn't, and so I have *had* to."

In sentence 4, what did Saroyan feel he had to do? Saroyan wrote this story as an adult. How do you think he felt about himself as an eleven-year-old? What makes you think so? Did you ever do anything when you were young that you were later very proud of or embarrassed about?

Saroyan comments about his uncle's talk with Miss Shenstone and Mr. Monsoon that, ". . . a brilliant man had come to my defense, a circumstance I could hardly be expected to enjoy." Why do you think he didn't enjoy the fact that his uncle helped him?

Composing

ranking

"Out of Order" and the passage from *Child of the Owl* both describe the relationship of a teacher and a student. You no doubt have formed an opinion about how good or bad the teacher and student in each story is. Your opinion reflects your beliefs about what makes a good teacher or student.

Begin this essay by describing the two characteristics that you think are the most essential to being an effective teacher. Then, explain your reasons for selecting the characteristics you have chosen. Finally, evaluate the teachers in each selection according to these characteristics. For example, if you believe that patience is one essential quality of a good teacher, how well do you think the teachers in these selections exemplify this characteristic? (Be sure to cite specific details from the text that show they either have or do not have this quality.)

Then, do the same thing for the students in the selections. Begin by describing what you believe are the two most important characteristics of a student and then evaluate each of the students on this basis.

photo: National Archives, Washington, D.C.

AND THE SOUL SHALL DANCE

Wakako Yamauchi

When many immigrants from Japan first came to the United States, they became truck farmers, who raised produce on small farms. On such farms, they were able to preserve many customs from Japan, including having a separate bathhouse with the water heated by wood fires. Very often a single man sent back to Japan for a wife he had never seen except in a picture.

IT'S ALL RIGHT TO TALK ABOUT IT NOW. Most of the principals are dead, except, of course, me and my younger brother, and possibly Kiyoko Oka, who might be near forty-five now, because, yes, I'm sure of it, she was fourteen then. I was nine, and my brother about four, so he hardly counts at all. Kiyoko's mother is dead, my father is dead, my mother is dead, and her father could not have lasted all these years with his tremendous appetite for alcohol and pickled chilies—those little yellow ones, so hot they could make your mouth hurt; he'd eat them like peanuts and tears would surge from his bulging thyroid eyes in great waves and stream down the dark coarse terrain of his face.

My father farmed then in the desert basin resolutely named Imperial Valley, in the township called Westmoreland; twenty acres of tomatoes, ten of summer squash, or vice versa, and the Okas lived maybe a mile, mile and a half, across an alkaline road, a stretch of greasewood, tumbleweed and white sand, to the south of us. We didn't hobnob much with them, because you see, they were a childless couple and we were a family: father, mother, daughter, and son, and we went to the Buddhist church on Sundays where my mother taught Japanese, and the Okas kept pretty much to themselves. I don't mean they were unfriendly; Mr. Oka would sometimes walk over (he rarely drove) on rainy days, all dripping wet, short and squat under a soggy newspaper, pretending to need a plow-blade or a file, and he would spend the afternoon in our kitchen drinking sake and eating chilies with my father. As he got progressively drunker, his large mouth would draw down and with the stream of tears, he looked like a kindly weeping bullfrog.

Not only were they childless, impractical in an area where large families were looked upon as labor potentials, but there was a certain strangeness about them. I became aware of it the summer our bathhouse burned down, and my father didn't get right down to building another, and a Japanese without a bathhouse . . . well, Mr. Oka offered us the use of his. So every night that summer we drove to the Okas for our bath, and we came in frequent contact with Mrs. Oka, and this is where I found the strangeness.

Mrs. Oka was small and spare. Her clothes hung on her like loose skin and when she walked, the skirt about her legs gave her a sort of webbed look. She was pretty in spite of the boniness and the dull calico and the barren look; I know now she couldn't have been over thirty. Her eyes were large and a little vacant, although once I saw them fill with tears; the time I insisted we take the old Victrola over and we played our Japanese records for her. Some of the songs were sad, and I imagined the nostalgia she felt, but my mother said the tears were probably from yawning or from the smoke of her cigarettes. I thought my mother resented her for not being more hospitable; indeed, never a cup of tea appeared before us, and between them the conversation of women was totally absent: the rise and fall of gentle voices, the arched eyebrows, the croon of polite surprise. But more than this, Mrs. Oka was *different*.

Obviously she was shy, but some nights she disappeared altogether. She would see us drive into her yard and then lurch from sight. She was gone all evening. Where could she have hidden in that two-roomed house—where in that silent desert? Some nights she would wait out our visit with enormous forbearance, quietly pushing wisps of stray hair behind her ears and waving gnats away from her great moist eyes, and some nights she moved about with nervous agitation, her khaki canvas shoes slapping loudly as she walked. And sometimes there appeared to be welts and bruises on her usually smooth brown face, and she would sit solemnly, hands on lap, eyes large and intent on us. My mother hurried us home then: "Hurry, Masako, no need to wash well; hurry."

You see, being so poky, I was always last to bathe. I think the Okas bathed after we left because my mother often reminded me to keep the water clean. The routine was to lather outside the tub (there were buckets and pans and a small wooden stool), rinse off the soil and soap, and then soak in the tub of hot hot water and contemplate. Rivulets of perspiration would run down the scalp.

When my mother pushed me like this, I dispensed with ritual, rushed a bar of soap around me and splashed about a pan of water. So hastily toweled, my wet skin trapped the clothes to me, impeding my already clumsy progress. Outside, my mother would be murmuring her many apologies and my father, I knew, would be carrying my brother whose feet were already sandy. We would hurry home.

I thought Mrs. Oka might be insane and I asked my mother about it, but she shook her head and smiled with her mouth drawn down and said that Mrs. Oka loved her sake. This was unusual, yes, but there were other unusual women we knew. Mrs. Nagai was bought by her husband from a geisha house; Mrs. Tani was a militant Christian Scientist; Mrs. Abe, the midwife, was occult. My mother's statement explained much: sometimes Mrs. Oka was drunk and sometimes not. Her taste for liquor and cigarettes was a step in the realm of men; unusual for a Japanese wife, but at that time, in that place, and to me, Mrs. Oka loved her sake in the way my father loved his, in the way of Mr. Oka, the way I loved my candy. That her psychology may have demanded this anesthetic, that she lived with something unendurable, did not occur to me. Nor did I perceive the violence of emotions that the purple welts indicated—or the masochism that permitted her to display these wounds to us.

In spite of her masculine habits, Mrs. Oka was never less than a woman. She was no lady in the area of social amenities; but the feminine in her was innate and never left her. Even in her disgrace, she was a small broken sparrow, slightly floppy, too slowly enunciating her few words, too carefully rolling her Bull Durham, cocking her small head and moistening the ocher tissue. Her aberration was a protest of the life assigned her; it was obstinate, but unobserved, alas, unheeded. "Strange" was the only concession we granted her.

Toward the end of summer, my mother said we couldn't continue bathing at the Okas'; when winter set in we'd all catch our death from the commuting and she'd always felt dreadful about our imposition on Mrs. Oka. So my father took the corrugated tin sheets he'd found on the highway and had been saving for some other use and built up our bathhouse again. Mr. Oka came to help.

While they raised the quivering tin walls, Mr. Oka began to talk. His voice was sharp and clear above the low thunder of the metal sheets.

He told my father he had been married in Japan previously to the present Mrs. Oka's older sister. He had a child by the marriage, Kiyoko, a girl. He had left the two to come to America intending to send for them soon, but shortly after his departure, his wife passed away from an obscure stomach ailment. At the time, the present Mrs. Oka was young and had foolishly become involved with a man of poor reputation. The family was anxious to part the lovers and conveniently arranged a marriage by proxy and sent him his dead wife's sister. Well that was all right, after all, they were kin, and it would be good for the child when she came to join them. But things didn't work out that way; year after year he postponed calling for his daughter, couldn't get the price of fare together, and the wife—ahhh, the wife, Mr. Oka's groan was lost in the rumble of his hammering.

He cleared his throat. The girl was now fourteen, he said, and begged to come to America to be with her own real family. Those relatives had forgotten the favor he'd done in accepting a slightly used bride, and now tormented his daughter for being forsaken. True, he'd not sent much money, but if they knew, if they only knew how it was here.

"Well," he sighed, "who could be blamed? It's only right she be with me anyway."

"That's right," my father said.

"Well, I sold the horse and some other things and managed to buy a third-class ticket on the Taiyo-Maru. Kiyoko will get here the first week of September." Mr. Oka glanced toward my father, but my father was peering into a bag of nails. "I'd be much obliged to you if your wife and little girl," he rolled his eyes toward me, "would take kindly to her. She'll be lonely."

Kiyoko-san came in September. I was surprised to see so very nearly a woman; short, robust, buxom: the female counterpart of her father; thyroid eyes and protruding teeth, straight black hair banded impudently into two bristly shucks, Cuban heels and white socks. Mr. Oka brought her proudly to us.

"Little Masako here," for the first time to my recollection, he touched me; he put his rough fat hand on the top of my head, "is very smart in school. She will help you with your school work, Kiyoko," he said.

I had so looked forward to Kiyoko-san's arrival. She would be my soul mate; in my mind I had conjured a girl of my own proportions: thin and tall, but with the refinement and beauty I didn't yet possess that would surely someday come to the fore. My disappointment was keen and apparent. Kiyoko-san stepped forward shyly, then retreated with a short bow and small giggle, her fingers pressed to her mouth.

My mother took her away. They talked for a long time—about Japan, about enrollment in American school, the clothes Kiyoko-san would need, and where to look for the best values. As I watched them, it occurred to me that I had been deceived: this was not a child, this was a woman. The smile pressed behind her fingers, the way of her nod, so brief, like my mother when father scolded her: the face was inscrutable, but something—maybe spirit—shrank visibly, like a piece of silk in water. I was disappointed; Kiyoko-san's soul was barricaded in her unenchanting appearance and the smile she fenced behind her fingers.

She started school from third grade, one below me, and as it turned out, she quickly passed me by. There wasn't much I could help her with except to drill her on pronunciation—the "L" and "R" sounds. Every morning walking to our rural school: land, leg, library, loan, lot; every afternoon returning home: ran, rabbit, rim, rinse, roll. That was the extent of our communication; friendly but uninteresting.

One particularly cold November night—the wind outside was icy; I was sitting on my bed, my brother's and mine, oiling the cracks in my chapped hands by lamplight—someone rapped urgently at our door. It was Kiyoko-san; she was hysterical, she wore no wrap, her teeth were chattering, and except for the thin straw zori, her feet were bare. My mother led her to the kitchen, started a pot of tea, and gestured to my brother and me to retire. I lay very still but because of my brother's restless tossing and my father's snoring, was unable to hear much. I was aware, though, that drunken and savage brawling had brought Kiyoko-san to us. Presently they came to the bedroom. I feigned sleep. My mother gave Kiyoko-san a gown and pushed me over to make room for her. My mother spoke firmly: "Tomorrow you will return to them; you must not leave them again. They are your people." I could almost feel Kiyoko-san's short nod.

All night long I lay cramped and still, afraid to intrude into her hulking back. Two or three times her icy feet jabbed into mine and quickly retreated. In the morning I found my mother's gown neatly folded on the spare pillow. Kiyoko-san's place in bed was cold.

She never came to weep at our house again but I know she cried: her eyes were often swollen and red. She stopped much of her giggling and routinely pressed her fingers to her mouth. Our daily pronunciation drill petered off from lack of interest. She walked silently with her shoulders hunched, grasping her books with both arms, and when I spoke to her in my halting Japanese, she absently corrected my prepositions.

Spring comes early in the Valley; in February the skies are clear though the air is still cold. By March, winds are vigorous and warm and wild flowers dot the desert floor, cockleburs are green and not yet tenacious, the sand is crusty underfoot, everywhere there is the smell of things growing and the first tomatoes are showing green and bald.

As the weather changed, Kiyoko-san became noticeably more cheerful. Mr. Oka who hated so to drive could often be seen steering his dusty old Ford over the road that passes our house, and Kiyoko-san sitting in front would sometimes wave gaily to us. Mrs. Oka was never with them. I thought of these trips as the westernizing of Kiyoko-san: with a permanent wave, her straight black hair became tangles of tiny frantic curls; between her textbooks she carried copies of *Modern Screen* and *Photoplay,* her clothes were gay with print and piping, and she bought a pair of brown suede shoes with alligator trim. I can see her now picking her way gingerly over the deceptive white peaks of alkaline crust.

At first my mother watched their coming and going with vicarious pleasure. "Probably off to a picture show; the stores are all closed at this hour," she might say. Later her eyes would get distant and she would muse, "They've left her home again; Mrs. Oka is alone again, the poor woman."

Now when Kiyoko-san passed by or came in with me on her way home, my mother would ask about Mrs. Oka—how is she, how does she occupy herself these rainy days, or these windy or warm or cool days. Often the answers were polite: "Thank you, we are fine," but sometimes Kiyoko-san's upper lip would pull over her teeth, and her voice would become very soft and she would say, "Drink, always drinking and fighting." At those times my mother would invariably say, "Endure, soon you will be marrying and going away."

Once a young truck driver delivered crates at the Oka farm and he dropped back to our place to tell my father that Mrs. Oka had lurched behind his truck while he was backing up, and very nearly let him kill her. Only the daughter pulling her away saved her, he said. Thoroughly unnerved, he stopped by to rest himself and talk about it. Never, never, he said in wide-eyed wonder, had he seen a drunken Japanese woman. My father nodded gravely, "Yes, it's unusual," he said and drummed his knee with his fingers.

Evenings were longer now, and when my mother's migraines drove me from the house in unbearable self-pity, I would take walks in the desert. One night with the warm wind against me, the dune primrose and yellow poppies closed and fluttering, the greasewood swaying in languid orbit, I lay on the white sand beneath a shrub and tried to disappear.

A voice sweet and clear cut through the half-dark of the evening:

Red lips press against a glass
Drink the purple wine
  And the soul shall dance

Mrs. Oka appeared to be gathering flowers. Bending, plucking, standing, searching, she added to a small bouquet she clasped. She held them away; looked at them slyly, lids lowered, demure, then in a sudden and sinuous movement, she broke into a stately dance. She stopped, gathered more flowers, and breathed deeply into them. Tossing her head, she laughed—softly, beautifully, from her dark throat. The picture of her imagined grandeur was lost to me, but the delusion that transformed the bouquet of tattered petals and sandy leaves, and the aloneness of a desert twilight into a fantasy that brought such joy and abandon made me stir with discomfort. The sound broke Mrs. Oka's dance. Her eyes grew large and her neck tense—like a cat on the prowl. She spied me in the bushes. A peculiar chill ran through me. Then abruptly and with childlike delight, she scattered the flowers around her and walked away singing:

Falling, falling, petals on a wind . . .

That was the last time I saw Mrs. Oka. She died before the spring harvest. It was pneumonia. I didn't attend the funeral, but my mother said it was sad. Mrs. Oka looked peaceful, and the minister expressed the irony of the long separation of Mother and Child and the short-lived reunion; hardly a year together, she said. We went to help Kiyoko-san address and stamp those black-bordered acknowledgements.

When harvest was over, Mr. Oka and Kiyoko-san moved out of the Valley. We never heard from them or saw them again and I suppose in a large city, Mr. Oka found some sort of work, perhaps as a janitor or a dishwasher and Kiyoko-san grew up and found someone to marry.

Exploring the Ideas

the plot

Indicate the order in which the following events occur in "And the Soul Shall Dance."

1. Masako's family drives to the Okas for their evening bath.
2. Kiyoko and her father go for a ride in their old Ford.
3. The bathhouse of Masako's family burns down.
4. The Okas move out of the Valley.
5. Mr. Oka's first wife dies.
6. Masako sees Mrs. Oka dancing.
7. Masako's father builds a new bathhouse.
8. Kiyoko comes to Masako's home on a cold November night.
9. Mr. Oka is married to the present Mrs. Oka's older sister.
10. The truck driver almost kills Mrs. Oka.
11. Mrs. Oka comes to America.
12. Mrs. Oka dies.
13. Kiyoko comes to America.

the characters

Indicate who is described in each of the following phrases: Mrs. Oka, Mr. Oka, Masako, or Kiyoko. If the description applies to more than one of them, indicate this by giving both names.

1. . . . was nine at the time of the story
2. . . . was fourteen at the time of the story
3. . . . was about thirty at the time of the story
4. . . . was small and spare
5. . . . was short, robust, and buxom
6. . . . had straight black hair
7. . . . sometimes had welts and bruises on her face
8. . . . had thyroid eyes and protruding teeth
9. . . . often had swollen and red eyes
10. . . . had curly black hair
11. . . . liked drinking sake
12. . . . liked eating chilies
13. . . . liked smoking

After reading the story you undoubtedly have formed an opinion about what type of person Mrs. Oka was. The following sentences describe Masako's opinion of Mrs. Oka. For each one indicate if you share the same opinion or if you have a different opinion.

- Mrs. Oka was strange.
- Mrs. Oka was nostalgic.
- Mrs. Oka was shy.
- Mrs. Oka was insane.

Give four more adjectives that you think describe Mrs. Oka. Then cite specific things from the text that show that she is that kind of person.

the theme

The story describes two Japanese families settling in America. For each sentence listed below indicate if their behavior seems to you to be typical of Japanese culture or unusual.

- The Okas are childless.
- Mrs. Oka never offers tea to her visitors.
- Mrs. Oka and Masako's mother never talk together.
- Mrs. Oka drinks sake.
- Mrs. Oka's family arranges a marriage by proxy.
- Mr. Oka does not send for Kiyoko for fourteen years.
- Kiyoko leaves her parents and comes to Masako's home.

1. The story begins with the statement, "It's all right to talk about it now." What does this statement suggest about the story that will follow?

2. Masako as the narrator of the story is no longer a child. As an adult, she comments in reference to Mrs. Oka's drinking: "That her psychology may have demanded this anesthetic, that she lived with something unendurable, did not occur to me." Why do you think Mrs. Oka drank?
3. Why do you think she would sometimes disappear when Masako's family came to bathe?
4. How do you think she got welts and bruises on her face? Why do you think she let Masako's family see them sometimes?
5. Why do you think she did not accompany Kiyoko and Mr. Oka on their drives in the old Ford?
6. Why do you think she got behind the truck?
7. Why do you think she danced in the desert?

Exploring the Language

sentence structure

The author has chosen to combine many sentences that are closely related into one longer sentence. Notice the following sentence:

"As I watched them, it occurred to me that I had been deceived: this was not a child, this was a woman."

This sentence could be rewritten into several short simple sentences as follows:

As I watched them, something occurred to me. I had been deceived. This was not a child. This was a woman.

Rewrite the following sentences into as many short simple sentences as possible.

1. "It was Kiyoko-san; she was hysterical, she wore no wrap, her teeth were chattering, and except for the thin straw zori, her feet were bare." (line 170)
2. "Toward the end of summer, my mother said we couldn't continue bathing at the Okas'; when winter set in we'd all catch our death from the commuting and she'd always felt dreadful about our imposition on Mrs. Oka." (line 97)

Why do you think the author has chosen to combine short simple sentences like those listed above into longer sentences? Pick out other sentences in the text that contain several simple sentences.

photo: courtesy the Port Authority of N.Y. & N.J.

PROLOGUE TO CALL IT SLEEP

Henry Roth

Call It Sleep *is a novel about Jewish immigrants to the United States. This excerpt is taken from the opening pages.*

Understanding the Language

There are terms in only the first two paragraphs with which you may be unfamiliar. If you read over these definitions first, you will be able to read the paragraphs more quickly.

The following terms are used in the first paragraph to describe the boat.

steerage—the section of a passenger ship near the rudder that often provides the cheapest accommodations
quay—the wharf where ships are loaded and unloaded
lee—the side of a ship that is sheltered from the wind, or any place sheltered from the wind
skipper—the master of a ship

The following terms are used in the second paragraph to describe the various types of immigrants.

joweled—heavy-jawed
scraggly—not orderly
docile—submissive
swarthy—dark-skinned
matrix—a network
gaudy—showy and tasteless
caftan—in the Middle East, a full-length tunic with long sleeves and a sash at the waist
gabardines—a suit made of wool or cotton
motley—of many colors
myriad—a large indefinite number

* * *

(I pray thee ask no questions
this is that Golden Land)

THE SMALL WHITE STEAMER, PETER STUYVESANT, that delivered the immigrants from the stench and throb of the steerage to the stench and the throb of New York tenements, rolled slightly on the water beside the stone quay in the lee of the weathered barracks and new brick buildings of Ellis Island. Her skipper was waiting for the last of the officials, laborers and guards to embark upon her before he cast off and started for Manhattan. Since this was Saturday afternoon and this the last trip she would make for the week-end, those left behind might have to stay over till Monday. Her whistle bellowed its hoarse warning. A few figures in overalls sauntered from the high doors of the immigration quarters and down the grey pavement that led to the dock.

It was May of the year 1907, the year that was destined to bring the greatest number of immigrants to the shores of the United States. All that day, as on all the days since spring began, her decks had been thronged by hundreds upon hundreds of foreigners, natives from almost every land in the world, the joweled close-cropped Teuton, the full-bearded Russian, the scraggly-whiskered Jew, and among them Slovack peasants with docile faces, smooth-cheeked and swarthy Armenians, pimply Greeks, Danes with wrinkled eyelids. All day her decks had been colorful, a matrix of the vivid costumes of other lands, the speckled green-and-yellow aprons, the flowered kerchief, embroidered homespun, the silver-braided sheepskin vest, the gaudy scarfs, yellow boots, fur caps, caftans, dull gabardines. All day the guttural, the high-pitched voices, the astonished cries, the gasps of wonder, reiterations of gladness had risen from her decks in a motley billow of sound. But now her decks were empty, quiet, spreading out under the sunlight almost as if the warm boards were relaxing from the strain and the pressure of the myriads of feet. All those steerage passengers of the ships that had docked that day who were permitted to enter had already entered—except two, a woman and a young child she carried in her arms. They had just come aboard escorted by a man.

About the appearance of these late comers there was very little that was unusual. The man had evidently spent some time in America and was now bringing his wife and child over from the other side. It might have been thought that he had spent most of his time in lower New York, for he paid only the scantest attention to the Statue of Liberty or to the city rising from the water or to the bridges spanning the East River—or perhaps he was merely too agitated to waste much time on these wonders. His clothes were the ordinary clothes the ordinary New Yorker wore in that period—sober and dull. A black derby accentuated the sharpness and sedentary pallor of his face; a jacket, loose on his tall spare frame, buttoned up in a V close to the throat; and above the V a tightly-knotted black tie was mounted in the groove of a high starched collar. As for his wife, one guessed that she was a European more by the timid wondering look in her eyes as she gazed from her husband to the harbor, than by her clothes. For her clothes were American—a black skirt, a white shirt-waist and a black jacket. Obviously her husband had either taken the precaution of sending them to her while she was still in Europe or had brought them with him to Ellis Island where she had slipped them on before she left.

Only the small child in her arms wore a distinctly foreign costume, an impression one got chiefly from the odd, outlandish, blue straw hat on his head with its polka dot ribbons of the same color dangling over each shoulder.

Except for this hat, had the three newcomers been in a crowd, no one probably, could have singled out the woman and child as newly arrived immigrants. They carried no sheets tied up in huge bundles, no bulky wicker baskets, no prized feather beds, no boxes of delicacies, sausages, virgin-olive oils, rare cheeses; the large black satchel beside them was their only luggage. But despite this, despite their even less than commonplace appearance, the two overalled men, sprawled out and smoking cigarettes in the stern, eyed them curiously. And the old peddler woman, sitting with basket of oranges on knee, continually squinted her weak eyes in their direction.

The truth was there was something quite untypical about their behavior. The old peddler woman on the bench and the overalled men in the stern had seen enough husbands meeting their wives and children after a long absence to know how such people ought to behave. The most volatile races, such as the Italians, often danced for joy, whirled each other around, pirouetted in an ecstasy: Swedes sometimes just looked at each other, breathing through open mouths like a panting dog; Jews wept, jabbered, almost put each other's eyes out with the recklessness of their darting gestures; Poles roared and gripped each other at arm's length as though they meant to tear a handful of flesh; and after one pecking kiss, the English might be seen gravitating toward, but never achieving an embrace. But these two stood silent, apart; the man staring with aloof, offended eyes grimly down at the water—or if he turned his face toward his wife at all, it was only to glare in harsh contempt at the blue straw hat worn by the child in her arms, and then his hostile eyes would sweep about the deck to see if anyone else were observing them. And his wife beside him regarding him uneasily, appealingly. And the child against her breast looking from one to the other with watchful, frightened eyes. Altogether it was a very curious meeting.

They had been standing in this strange and silent manner for several minutes, when the woman, as if driven by the strain into action, tried to smile, and touching her husband's arm said timidly, "And this is the Golden Land." She spoke in Yiddish.

The man grunted, but made no answer.

She took a breath as if taking courage, and tremulously, "I'm sorry, Albert, I was so stupid." She paused waiting for some flicker of unbending, some word, which never came. "But you look so lean, Albert, so haggard. And your mustache—you've shaved."

His brusque glance stabbed and withdrew. "Even so."

"You must have suffered in this land." She continued gentle despite his rebuke. "You never wrote me. You're thin. Ach! Then here in the new land is the same old poverty. You've gone without food. I can see it. You've changed."

"Well that don't matter," he snapped, ignoring her sympathy. "It's no excuse for your not recognizing me. Who else would call for you? Do you know anyone else in this land?"

"No," placatingly. "But I was so frightened, Albert. Listen to me. I was so bewildered, and that long waiting there in that vast room since morning. Oh, that horrible waiting! I saw them all go, one after the other. The shoemaker and his wife. The coppersmith and his children from Strij. All those on the Kaiserin Viktoria. But I—I remained. Tomorrow will be Sunday. They told me no one could come to fetch me. What if they sent me back? I was frantic!"

"Are you blaming me?" His voice was dangerous.

"No! No! Of course not Albert! I was just explaining."

"Well then let me explain," he said curtly. "I did what I could. I took the day off from the shop. I called that cursed Hamburg-American Line four times. And each time they told me you weren't on board."

"They didn't have any more third-class passage, so I had to take the steerage—"

"Yes, now I know. That's all very well. That couldn't be helped. I came here anyway. The last boat. And what do you do? You refused to recognize me. You don't know me." He dropped his elbows down on the rail, averted his angry face. "That's the greeting I get."

"I'm sorry, Albert," she stroked his arm humbly. "I'm sorry."

"And as if those blue-coated mongrels in there weren't mocking me enough, you give them that brat's right age. Didn't I write you to say seventeen months because it would save the half fare! Didn't you hear me inside when I told them?"

"How could I, Albert?" she protested. "How could I? You were on the other side of that—that cage."

"Well why didn't you say seventeen months anyway? Look!" he pointed to several blue-coated officials who came hurrying out of a doorway out of the immigration quarters. "There they are." An ominous pride dragged at his voice. "If he's among them, that one who questioned me so much, I could speak to him if he came up here."

"Don't bother with him, Albert," she exclaimed uneasily. "Please, Albert! What have you against him? He couldn't help it. It's his work."

"Is it?" His eyes followed with unswerving deliberation the bluecoats as they neared the boat. "Well he didn't have to do it so well."

"And after all, I did lie to him, Albert," she said hurriedly trying to distract him.

"The truth is you didn't," he snapped, turning his anger against her. "You made your first lie plain by telling the truth afterward. And made a laughing-stock of me!"

"I didn't know what to do." She picked despairingly at the wire grill beneath the rail. "In Hamburg the doctor laughed at me when I said seventeen months. He's so big. He was big when he was born." She smiled, the worried look on her face vanishing momentarily as she stroked her son's cheek. "Won't you speak to your father, David, beloved?"

The child merely ducked his head behind his mother.

His father stared at him, shifted his gaze and glared down at the officials, and then, as though perplexity had crossed his mind he frowned absently. "How old did he say he was?"

"The doctor? Over two years—and as I say he laughed."

"Well what did he enter?"

"Seventeen months—I told you."

"Then why didn't you tell them seventeen—" He broke off, shrugged violently. "Baah! You need more strength in this land." He paused, eyed her intently and then frowned suddenly. "Did you bring his birth certificate?"

"Why—" She seemed confused. "It may be in the trunk—there on the ship. I don't know. Perhaps I left it behind." Her hand wandered uncertainly to her lips. "I don't know. Is it important? I never thought of it. But surely father could send it. We need only write."

"Hmm! Well, put him down." His head jerked brusquely toward the child. "You don't need to carry him all the way. He's big enough to stand on his own feet."

She hesitated, and then reluctantly set the child down on the deck. Scared, unsteady, the little one edged over to the side opposite his father, and hidden by his mother, clung to her skirt.

"Well, it's all over now." She attempted to be cheerful. "It's all behind us now, isn't it, Albert? Whatever mistakes I made don't really matter any more. Do they?"

"A fine taste of what lies before me!" He turned his back on her and leaned morosely against the rail. "A fine taste!"

They were silent. . . .

The western wind whipped the polka-dot ribbons on the child's hat straight out behind him. They caught his father's eye.

"Where did you find that crown?"

Startled by his sudden question his wife looked down. "That? That was Maria's parting gift. The old nurse. She bought it herself and then sewed the ribbons on. You don't think it's pretty?"

"Pretty? Do you still ask?" His lean jaws hardly moved as he spoke. "Can't you see that those idiots lying back there are watching us already? They're mocking us! What will the others do on the train? He looks like a clown in it. He's the cause of all this trouble anyway!"

The harsh voice, the wrathful glare, the hand flung toward the child frightened him. Without knowing the cause, he knew that the stranger's anger was directed at himself. He burst into tears and pressed closer to his mother.

"Quiet!" the voice above him snapped.

Cowering, the child wept all the louder.

"Hush, darling!" His mother's protecting hands settled on his shoulders.

"Just when we're about to land!" her husband said furiously "He begins this! This howling! And now we'll have it all the way home, I suppose! Quiet! You hear?"

"It's you who are frightening him, Albert!" she protested.

"Am I? Well, let him be quiet. And take that straw gear off his head."

"But Albert, it's cool here."

"Will you take that off when I—" A snarl choked whatever else he would have uttered. While his wife looked on aghast, his long fingers scooped the hat from the child's head. The next instant it was sailing over the ship's side to the green waters below. The overalled men in the stern grinned at each other. The old orange-peddler shook her head and clucked.

"Albert!" his wife caught her breath. "How could you?"

"I could!" he rapped out. "You should have left it behind!" His teeth clicked, and he glared about the deck.

She lifted the sobbing child to her breast, pressed him against her. With a vacant stunned expression, her gaze wandered from the grim smouldering face of her husband to the stern of the ship. In the silvery-green wake that curved trumpet-wise through the water, the blue hat still bobbed and rolled, ribbon stretched out on the waves. Tears sprang to her eyes. She brushed them away quickly, shook her head as if shaking off the memory, and looked toward the bow. Before her the grimy cupolas and towering square walls of the city loomed up. Above the jagged roof tops, the white smoke, whitened and suffused by the slanting sun, faded into the slots and wedges of the sky. She pressed her brow against her child's, hushed him with whispers. This was that vast incredible land, the land of freedom, of immense opportunity, that Golden Land. Again she tried to smile.

"Albert," she said timidly, "Albert."

"Hm?"

"Gehen vir voinen du? In Nev York?"

"Nein. Bronzeville. Ich hud dir schoin geschriben."

She nodded uncertainly, sighed . . .

Screws threshing, backing water, the Peter Stuyvesant neared her dock—drifting slowly and with canceled momentum as if reluctant.

Exploring the Ideas

the setting

The first several paragraphs provide the details of the setting. Indicate those details that you think are an accurate description of the setting and those that you think are inaccurate. Then correct those that are inaccurate.

1. The steamer was docked in New York harbor.
2. The ship was waiting to leave Ellis Island.
3. This was the first trip of the weekend.
4. Some of the last people to board the ship were immigration officials.
5. It was the spring of the year.
6. The passengers came from a variety of countries.
7. All day the deck had been empty and quiet.
8. All of the passengers were dressed in a similar fashion.
9. All of the steerage passengers had already entered.

point of view

The narrator of the story is like a camera. He can observe all of the characters, but he does not know what they are thinking. Nevertheless, he makes several inferences about the characters. Indicate those things that the narrator can actually observe and those things that he infers from their behavior or appearance.

1. The man had spent most of his time in lower New York.
2. The man wore typical clothes for New York for that period.
3. The woman was European.
4. The man had either sent the woman her clothes or given them to her on Ellis Island.
5. The boy was a foreigner.

6. The boy wore an unusual blue straw hat.
7. The family carried only a large black satchel for luggage.
8. The man and woman stood silent and apart.
9. The man stared at the water.
10. The man glared at the blue straw hat.
11. The wife looked at her husband uneasily.
12. The child looked watchful and frightened.
13. The woman touched the man's arm and spoke to him in Yiddish.

relationships

Why did the narrator think that the reunion of this family was strange? How did Italian relatives often greet one another? Swedish? Jewish? Polish? English?

What is the first thing the wife says to her husband? She then apologizes to her husband for being stupid and not recognizing him. What excuse does she give for her mistake? Does her husband forgive her? What is the husband's excuse for not arriving on time?

The husband is angry at what the wife tells the immigration official. He calls them mongrels or dogs. What does he call the boy? What was the wife supposed to tell the immigration officials about the boy? Why was she supposed to do this? How old is the child?

The following are quotations of what the man says to his wife. For each one describe how he should say the line if he were an actor in a film based on this novel.

Example

Quotation: He says to his wife about her not recognizing him first: "I came here anyway. The last boat. And what do you do? You refused to recognize me." (line 120)
Tone of voice: unsympathetic, accusing

1. He tells his wife about her lie: You made "a laughing-stock of me!" (line 145)
2. He says to his wife in reference to her not repeating the lie: "You need more strength in this land." (line 160)
3. He says to his wife about the child: "Well, put him down. You don't need to carry him all the way. He's big enough to stand on his own feet." (line 167)
4. When the child starts to cry he says: "Just when we're about to land! He begins this! This howling! And now we'll have it all the way home, I suppose! Quiet! You hear?" (line 197)

5. He says in reference to the child's hat: "Will you take that off. . ." (line 204)

What adjective do you think best describes the man?
What do you think the wife says to the husband in the dialogue in Yiddish? The actual translation is the following:

"Are we going to live there? In New York?"

"No, in Bronzeville. I have already written to you."

Is this similar to what you guessed?

How would you describe the relationship of the husband and wife? Why do you think they have this kind of relationship?

Exploring the Language

descriptive language

In order to give the reader a concrete image of the scene, Henry Roth provides many exact details. For example, he lists specific items—aprons, kerchiefs, vests, etc.—that are on the deck. Consult the text to answer the following questions.

characters

What color were the husband's clothes? Did he have a hat? A jacket? A tie? What type of shirt was he wearing?

What was the wife wearing?

What were the two men on the deck wearing? What were they doing?

What was the peddler woman doing?

objects

How were the barracks different from the buildings of Ellis Island? Does the picture of Ellis Island show the difference?

What was the hat that the child was wearing like?

What was the city that they were approaching like? Look at the selection from *West Side Story* for a fairly modern picture of New York.

dialogue

A great deal of the chapter is devoted to relating what the characters say. In introducing the dialogue, Henry Roth frequently makes use of verbs and adverbs to indicate *how* the words were spoken. Use the clues from *what* is said to match the meaning of the underlined verb or adverb with the following definitions.

1. "They had been standing in this strange and silent manner for several minutes, when the woman, as if driven by strain into action, tried to smile, and touching her husband's arm said timidly, 'And this is the Golden Land.'" (line 88)
2. "The man grunted, but made no answer.
   "She took a breath as if taking courage, and tremulously, 'I'm sorry, Albert, I was so stupid.'" (line 92)
3. "'You must have suffered in this land.'" She continued gentle despite his rebuke. 'You never wrote me. You're thin. Ach! Then here in the new land is the same old poverty. You've gone without food. I can see it. You've changed.'
   "'Well that don't matter,' he snapped, ignoring her sympathy." (line 98)
4. "'It's no excuse for your not recognizing me. Who else would call for you? Do you know anyone else in this land?'"
   "'No' placatingly. 'But I was so frightened, Albert.'" (line 103)
5. "'Are you blaming me?'" His voice was dangerous.
   "'No! No! Of course not Albert! I was just explaining.'
   "'Well then let me explain,' he said curtly." (line 112)
6. "'And as if those blue-coated mongrels in there weren't mocking me enough, you give them that brat's right age. Didn't I write you to say seventeen months because it would save the half fare! Didn't you hear me inside when I told them?'
   "'How could I, Albert?' she protested. 'How could I? You were on the other side of that—that cage.'" (line 125)
7. "Cowering, the child wept all the louder.
   "'Hush, darling!' His mother's protecting hands settled on his shoulders.
   "'Just when we're about to land!' her husband said furiously 'He begins this! This howling!'" (line 194)
8. "While his wife looked on aghast, his long fingers scooped the hat from the child's head. The next instant it was sailing over the ship's side to the green waters below. . . .
   "'Albert!' his wife caught her breath. 'How could you?'"
   "'I could!' He rapped out.'" (line 205)

Definitions

a. angrily
b. calmly so as to appease anger
c. fearfully
d. rudely
e. shyly
f. to object
g. to speak sharply
h. to utter in a sharp manner

Composing

comparing/contrasting

"The Soul Shall Dance" and *Call It Sleep* both depict a husband, wife, and child in the New World. In both cases the family life is far from ideal. In this essay compare and contrast the families in these selections. Consider the following questions.

1. In what way did immigrating to a new land cause problems for the Okas? For the family in *Call It Sleep*?
2. How would you characterize the relationship of Mr. and Mrs. Oka? Of the couple in *Call It Sleep*? Does the husband or wife in either case try to create a good relationship?
3. How would you characterize the relationship of Mr. Oka and Kiyoko in "The Soul Shall Dance"? Of the father and child in *Call It Sleep*? Of the mother and the child in "The Soul Shall Dance"? In *Call It Sleep*?

One way to organize the essay is to describe the Oka family and then compare and contrast it with the family in *Call It Sleep*. A second possibility is to deal with a specific category such as the parent-child relationship in "The Soul Shall Dance" and *Call It Sleep* and then deal with another category such as the husband-wife relationship.

speculating

As readers, we often make predictions while we are reading as to what will happen in a story. After we have finished reading a story, we might speculate as to what would have happened if the plot had been slightly altered or the characters had acted differently. In these essays you will be asked to speculate and make predictions.

Choose either Topic I or Topic II:

TOPIC I. At the end of "The Soul Shall Dance" Masako speculates that Mr. Oka had found some work and Kiyoko-san had gotten married. In this essay, speculate how the life of Mr. Oka, Mrs. Oka and Kiyoko-san might have been different if Kiyoko-san had never come to America. Consider the following questions.

1. Do you think Mr. and Mrs. Oka would have continued to drink?
2. Do you think Mr. and Mrs. Oka might have started taking rides in the old Ford?
3. Do you think Mrs. Oka would have jumped in front of the truck? Would have danced and gathered flowers in the desert?
4. Do you think Mr. and Mrs. Oka would have moved out of the Valley?

Be sure to cite specific things in the text that led you to your conclusion.

TOPIC II. The passage from *Call It Sleep* is the first chapter of the novel. In the chapter we are briefly introduced to the three main characters. Based on the information that you have, predict what the life of this family will be like in America. Consider the following questions.

1. Where do you imagine they will live?
2. Where do you think the father will work?
3. How quickly do you think the wife and child will learn English?
4. What kind of relationship do you think the husband and wife will have? The father and son? The mother and son?

Wherever possible, use specific facts from the story that led you to your conclusion.

photo: Irene Springer.

"PROSPECTIVE IMMIGRANTS PLEASE NOTE"

Adrienne Rich

Either you will
go through this door
or you will not go through.

If you go through
there is always the risk
of remembering your name.

Things look at you doubly
and you must look back
and let them happen.

If you do not go through
it is possible
to live worthily

to maintain your attitudes
to hold your position
to die bravely

but much will blind you,
much will evade you,
at what cost who knows?

The door itself
makes no promises.
It is only a door.

Exploring the Ideas

Who, of all the people you have read about so far, do you think have gone through the door? Which of them have remembered their name?

Who have not gone through the door? What do you think might have prevented them?

APPENDIX

The following is a list of the composition topics included in the text. Listed below each topic is a summary of which exercises in McKay, *Fundamentals of Writing for a Specific Purpose* (Englewood Cliffs, N.J.: Prentice-Hall, 1983) will provide practice in relevant grammatical and rhetorical structures for the essay.

describing a place — page 8

The exercises on prepositions with expressions of place and descriptive adjectives of place in the chapter, "Describing a Place."

describing a personality — page 17

The exercises on pronoun reference, nonrestrictive relative clauses, relevancy of support, descriptive adjectives, and the peer correction of student compositions in the chapter, "Describing a Personality."

describing an event — pages 3, 34

The exercises on verb tense, adverbial clauses of time, and participial phrases in the chapter, "Describing an Event."

defining by example — page 54

The exercises on parallel structure with infinitives and gerunds and on sentence connectors of exemplification in the chapter, "Defining by Example." The exercises on expressions of opinion and statements of reason in the chapter, "Expressing and Supporting an Opinion."

describing a place — page 65

The exercises on descriptive adjectives of place in the chapter, "Describing a Place." The expressions of opinion and statements of reason in the chapter, "Expressing and Supporting an Opinion."

classifying effects page 66

The exercises on the use of the colon to introduce categories, sentence connectors of classification, and dividing a topic and categorizing data in the chapter, "Defining by Classification." The exercises on expressions of cause and effect in the chapter, "Speculating."

comparing/contrasting pages 82, 91, 103, 136

The sentence connectors of comparison and contrast in the chapter, "Defining by Comparison and Contrast."

describing a place and the people page 97

The exercises on prepositions with expressions of place and descriptive adjectives of place in the chapter, "Describing a Place." Also the exercises on pronoun reference, expressions of quantity, relative clauses, and descriptive adjectives in the chapter, "Describing a Personality."

expressing opinions page 97

The exercises on subordinate clauses, expressions of opinion, and statements of reason in the chapter, "Expressing an Opinion."

ranking page 114

The exercises on subordinate clauses and expressions of opinion in the chapter, "Expressing an Opinion." The exercises on cleft sentences, parallel structure, and the reading selection in the chapter, "Ranking."

speculating page 136

The exercises on conditional sentences, ways of expressing hypothetical situations, and expressions of cause and effect in the chapter, "Speculating."